21st Century Hotel

21st Century Hotel

Graham Vickers

Laurence King Publishing

LAURENCE KING

Published in 2005 by
Laurence King Publishing Ltd
71 Great Russell Street
London WC1B 3BP
T: +44 (0)20 7430 8850
F: +44 (0)20 7430 8880
E: -enquiries@laurenceking.co.uk
www.laurenceking.co.uk

A catalogue record for this book is available from the
British Library.

ISBN 1 85669 401 1

Printed in Singapore

Project managed by Lara Maiklem
Designed by Price Watkins

Contents

184 Architectural Significance

Introduction

'The Station Hotel?... It's a building of small architectural merit built for some unknown purpose at the turn of the century. It was converted into a hotel by public subscription. I stayed there once myself as a young man. It has a reputation for luxury that baffles the most undemanding guest.'

Dr. Prentice in *What The Butler Saw* by Joe Orton.

The phrase '21st-century-hotel design' inevitably has a touch of the futuristic about it, something light years away from Joe Orton's ominously recognizable Station Hotel. True, we are already living in that twenty-first century, but there remains a sense of impersonal progress about the phrase, almost as though hotel design strides ahead and those of us who actually stay in hotels must somehow try to keep up with the trends. In fact, the exact opposite is true. Hotels have never been so earnestly responsive to the Zeitgeist – or at least what hotel operators, owners, developers and designers perceive to be the Zeitgeist. How else can we explain the latest trends in hotel design, which at one extreme increasingly blur the border between lodging, lifestyle, refuge and living theatre, and at the other still seek continue to reinvent the more discreet manners and style of the grand hotels of the past?

This book seeks to explore some of the latest trends and ideas in a sector that has often experienced some difficulty in finding appropriate descriptive terms for the many different shades of hotel experience on offer all over the world. Part of this difficulty derives directly from the worldwide nature of business travel and tourism. Although local notions of luxury in Mexico City are not necessarily the same as those in Manhattan, now that international travel has homogenized our expectations of comfort and service, it is often left to international 'design', in the broadest sense of the word, to add the distinction, variety and shading that local manners would once have imposed, and to project the hotel's image into a market place that now embraces the borderless Internet.

Trends are much harder to pin down than might be imagined. The practising experts – designers, architects, developers and owners – who might be considered to be the most involved and therefore the most informed observers of hotel design, usually turn out to have a vested interest, and seek to extrapolate

from their own latest venture evidence that this is indeed the exact shape of things to come. Perhaps more unguardedly revealing is the wealth of promotional copy generated by the marketing companies whose task it is to sell certain types of new hotel to the public. Someone once remarked, after a disastrous gastronomic tour of the United States, that he now knew the one thing that American restaurants did really well: the menu. Similarly, the overripe *cartes du jour* issuing from those who market particular kinds of hotel seem intent upon making them sound like Lourdes, Shangri-La and Eldorado all rolled into one. The chasm between promise and reality is ludicrous but in certain cases pretence and pretension may be camouflaged, or at least diminished, by interior design or architecture of considerable quality.

What then does this tell us? That there seems to be a growing public appetite for hotels masquerading as health farms and spiritual retreats and that some quite distinguished hotel designers are cheerful accomplices in fashionable bids to realize them. It tells us why every other hotel must now have its spa, a word suddenly divested of its true meaning and commercially re-coined by the hotel industry to mean any sort of indoor water feature with a press agent. It tells us, too, that any hotel fortunate enough to be surrounded by dramatic natural beauty would do well to investigate every local peak, crag and rill for regional evidence of spiritual history and then promptly install a totemic crystal energy chamber before publicizing itself as a time-honoured retreat for burnt-out movers and shakers.

More interestingly, these excesses have filtered down to make more sober health and fitness facilities (often with their vaguely defined overtones of 'well-being' and 'purification') *de rigueur* at almost all new hotels, cutting across every category with the exception of those budget establishments unable to provide any non-essential services at all.

Looking Back, Looking Forward

What of those categories? The main ones adopted in this book are admittedly loose groupings but also, one hopes, helpful ones. The idea of reinterpreting tradition is an enduring and fascinating one, calling for very precise readings of contemporary perspectives on the past. Every age throws up popular culture versions of a past period. To take just one example, an epic eleven-part 1980s UK television version of *Brideshead Revisited* fixed the visual and social manners of inter-war British aristocracy for a whole generation and, incidentally, still exerts its influence today, leading a London hotelier to describe his new establishment as *Brideshead Revisited* meets *Sex and the City*. This is a cultural get-together about which one feels Evelyn Waugh might have had something to say, despite the fact that it is the television series not the novel that is being referred to. In short, tradition is a media-mediated moveable feast from which the passing moment picks and chooses.

The hotels featured in the *Traditional Reinterpretations* section of this book can therefore be seen to be reinventing very selective elements from the built past for a modern consumer. This consumer's visual sophistication is certainly greater than ever before, but he or she is also more heavily influenced by a wealth of manipulated images of the past that have been created by film and television. Tradition, or the illusion of it, may bring reassurance but people also want the manners of the past to be invisibly blended with the benefits of today; they are certainly smart enough to know that a Las Vegas' desert recreation of Venice is a joke and not a reinterpretation. To cater for such a clientele, designers and architects must avoid pastiche and create, instead, a much subtler synthesis of tradition.

Mass Appeal

By definition most mainstream hotels have always been more concerned with reflecting style rather than actually setting it. However, today even the mainstream cannot afford to fall too far behind when it comes to design credibility. *Mainstream Experiments*, therefore, considers some hotels that have sought to combine the established image of the business, tourist or luxury hotel with fresh design thinking that unmistakeably hooks them into the spirit of the times without alienating guests who may still seek the familiar reassurance – and sometimes the omnipresent corporate-style hallmark – of the trusted hotel chain.

Here, the prevailing trend seems to be one of trying to square the circle between corporate control and a more informal, independent-looking presence in the market place. Much of the evidence suggests that the balance will tip in favour of loosely branded individual identities as the big chains start to ape Ian Schrager's now legendary recipe for success: buying up existing hotels that have been under-marketed or under-branded and using well-judged design to help them to shed their faceless images in favour of an attractive new variety of carefully managed individualism.

Oddballs and Auteurs

No such balancing acts trouble either the designer hotel or the kind of hotel that has been conceived for a unique purpose or founded upon an attention-grabbing gimmick. *Designer Hotels* deals with seven design experiments that can be further subdivided.

Manhattan's Soho House benefits from the attentions of a designer, Ilse Crawford, who is herself something of a minor jet-set celebrity. The result is an almost perfect synthesis of real visual style and celebrity buzz, a latter-day equivalent of the rather more austere cachet once enjoyed by, say, Boston's Parker Hotel when Charles Dickens used to stay there. Today, no one wants to stay at a hotel where some long-dead famous person once lodged, if only because the place's corresponding antiquity is likely to raise grave doubts about things like plumbing and the telecommunications. What trendy, up-to-the-minute guests really want to hear is that famously fussy divas like Diana Ross or Barbra Streisand occupied their hotel of choice just last month.

For those who like their *avant-garde* design undiluted, HI Hotel in Nice typifies what happens when a designer is given an unconditional licence to reinvent the possibilities of a hotel. Staying at this establishment is not for the faint-hearted but rather for those who want to align themselves with modish experiments in organizing living space with surreal adventures in room role-reversal or other demanding hospitality experiences. Most of these 'experiments' are unlikely to be welcomed by a weary businessman who is simply looking for a bar that doesn't resemble a James Bond film set and a bed that doesn't turn into a bath.

Some premises resist the attentions of even the most dedicated designer, as an old American Legion building in Paris illustrates. Andrée Putman, past mistress of the Big Hotel Design Push of the 1980s, has certainly done enough to make this old building into a new hotel with a certain touch of class but conservation considerations limited her interventions, perhaps more than she would have liked. Putman's peer in the 80s designer revolution was Philippe Starck whose unmistakeable stamp can be seen all over a venerable San Francisco hotel, also featured in this chapter. Here, though, the treatment is unexpectedly Post Modern and the book's only example of what is now seen as a rather passé style, saved by Starck's continuing ability to invest his arch quotations from the past with real quality, style and wit as well as a welcome sense of the unexpected.

Original Ideas spans two areas of activity: serious purpose and playful theming. By definition, each hotel that is dealt with in this section needs to be discussed on its own terms, but what general lesson, if any, can we draw from the one-off hotel? When the starting point is the rational one of a design that aims to addresses a unique set of circumstances, probably none. But when the Unique Selling Proposition is an assumed one, it usually has something to do with the burgeoning idea of the hotel as sort of fantasy camp.

Want to get married in an ice palace? Fancy the erotic literature suite of a hotel tricked out like a library? Feel like being born again in a stylized Tyrolean retreat? If so, then you are probably the sort of person who feels more comfortable with a leisure experience that has been carefully branded by someone else. Depending on your point of view, this can be a potentially disquieting idea, not altogether unrelated to the notion of dubbing canned laughter onto the soundtrack of a television show in order to tell audiences when they ought to find something funny. But even when the guests take such hotels less seriously than the hoteliers do, the underlying trend spills over into other, less obviously 'original' hotel concepts. Even a modest (if inventive) reinterpretation of an old budget hotel in downtown Tokyo now offers to provide its guests with 'many answers to the question how to live'. There is a specific cultural undertow that can be seen at work here that, whether overtly or subliminally, increasingly seeks to align a hotel stay with theatre, therapy or even treatment.

Historically, of course, there was always an element of this in the stereotypical Grand Hotel; with its sweeping staircases, lavish restaurants and theatrical public spaces, it was a place for society people to see and be seen. The difference was that there was no themed agenda, no communal psychological purpose and no expectation of anything other than a glittering upscale setting for social dramas. Today, however, the dominant trend is for themed hotels to provide not only the drama but the setting as well.

Building the Dream

It is also true, though, that this growth of the themed hotel experience has been stimulated by factors more pragmatic than psychosocial nuances. The global economic cycle will always condition the amount of new building taking place at a given time and a recent shortage of new-build hotels has necessarily pushed hotel design activity more into the province of the interior designer – who may be asked or tempted to create dramatic themes – than the architect. In addition to this, stringent planning regulation can place considerable restrictions upon the design possibilities of any new hotel that does get built, further shifting the onus of making a strong and distinctive visual statement upon interior design.

Yet common sense tells us that the best hotel design will always be holistic: the building envelope will make the major design statement and, with luck, the interior

will follow it through. Making the structure the starting point can therefore put the whole design process into a more leisurely time frame, militating against the kind of excesses that come from short-term fashion-led thinking and rapid execution. This can be a benefit from the point of view of restraint but may prove a disadvantage if the business plan demands a brisker timetable. In the best cases, good architecture may bring a level of quality to hotel design that nothing else can. Thus, *Architectural Significance* draws together some exemplary hotel projects where the building sets the agenda and interaction between interior and exterior is of exceptional interest.

A new Radisson hotel for the city of Glasgow might also have qualified for inclusion in *Mainstream Experiments* but it is its architectural impact that is so strong as to provide the primary focus of interest. Here, a whole design approach is flagged by the building itself, which successfully juggles with a range of practical issues and restrictions to create a strong statement reflecting something of the spirit of Glasgow and its history without ever being overly reverential or resorting to pastiche. The boldness of this particular piece of hotel architecture has also attracted some other good designers to create facilities inside as well as determining the architects' own treatment of the internal public spaces. Only the standardized, 'cookie-cutter' Radisson guest room design remains untouched by the inventive spirit of the building.

Eva Jiricna's Hotel Josef in Prague is an exceptionally satisfying hotel building, respectful of its surroundings, light in its visual references and very far removed from the sort of hotel that wants to rent out a lifestyle to its guests. Meanwhile, the elaborate architectural story behind Austria's Parkhotel is worth a small book of its own, but even the shortest account reveals how architectural restitution and a proper regard for site and history can result in the most surprising and enjoyable contemporary hotel design solution. In Mexico City, an old industrial building arms itself against an abrasive locale with a stunning new glass outer skin. In Rome, a new hotel building tries to elevate its run-down surroundings simply by being there. In São Paulo, a master architect with a bold agenda uses giant curved building blocks to illustrate how a hotel might look if it didn't have to look like a hotel. And, in what would once have once been called the American West's Indian country, a spa complex with spiritual and mystical aspirations gets an architectural treatment that takes an insubstantial agenda very seriously.

Without exception, these architectural solutions are solving problems that are way over and above the normal ones that attend the design of any building: they are giving solid form, not a coat of paint, to a hotelier's dream. Whether it falls to the architects themselves or to others to flesh out the interior, in most cases the best possible start has been made.

Hotels for Consumers

As indicated earlier, hotel operators, owners, developers and designers seem never to have been quite so earnestly responsive to the spirit of the times... or at least what they understand to be the spirit of the times. Certainly, at the start of the 21st century, our tastes are changing faster than ever. Lifestyles, cars, clothes, consumer products and the media shift and transform their complexion almost as fast as the digital technology that increasingly underpins them and most other aspects of 21st-century life.

Hotels have joined the fray and, despite the occasional example where residential rooms and suites have been installed in order to offset the financial unpredictability of hotel room rentals, the modern hotel seems, in general, to be in the throes of acquiring the same kind of transitory permanence that is already enjoyed by theatres, cinemas and restaurants. This is to say that the institution endures but its ever-changing menu of experiences on offer is intended to keep it fresh and ensure repeat business.

The days when people would return, year after year, to the same hotel in the same vacation resort precisely because it was unchanging now seem very distant. So too does the notion of the permanent hotel guest who maintains a room or a suite in perpetuity instead of a regular home. In the Coen Brothers' movie *Barton Fink*, set in the 1940s, the East Coast playwright hero arrives in a daze at the Hotel Earle, the sort of Los Angeles hotel one would not wish on one's worst enemy. At reception he is presented with a register to sign and a baffling

question to answer: '...are you a tranz or a rez?' This means is he registering as a transient or a resident, the bell captain explains. The hotel's motto reads 'Hotel Earle: A Day or a Lifetime'. He does not know what to put; his stay will be indefinite.

Today, the implied question, tranz or rez, becomes ever less relevant to the hotel experience. The hotel as home from home, just like the hotel as temporary lodging, is no longer the automatic way we think of hotels or the way hotels think of themselves. Some may still fulfil these roles but that is not where the key to commercial success lies. Tourism is one of the world's fastest-growing industries and, as a result of this, hotels are becoming destinations in themselves. A big designer name can still guarantee column inches in the world's press and, to some extent, all hotels are now getting into show business; their guests, neither tranz nor rez, are instead sophisticated consumers of experiences: plays, movies, meals, hotel stays.

Quite apart from the role of star designer as publicity magnet, the role of design itself has now become central to defining, shading and colouring the continually shifting choice of what hotels offer us. All the signs are that this process is here to stay and that it will continue to be the designer who provides the vital connecting tissue between the ambitions of the hotel developer and the dreams of the consumer. That consumer, unlike the baffled guests at Orton's Station Hotel, is anything but undemanding and can not only tell the difference between bogus luxury and the real thing, but also appreciate and enjoy many intermediary shades of hospitality experience as well.

1 Traditional Reinterpretations

Few 21st-century hotel guests would be satisfied with the standards of hospitality that prevailed 50 years ago, and yet a popular appetite for the trappings of the past endures. This may show itself in a variety of ways: in pastiches of antique design and decoration; in the notion of old-style deferential service; or in the sort of hotel that embodies a quality and style that exceeds the standards its guests normally enjoy at home. If this sounds out of step with contemporaneous trends, where hotels become fantasy camps, style clubs or health farms, it should be remembered that the traditionalism being evoked is of a type largely informed by popular culture, not historical record. Thus a hotel based on the image of the classic English country house can still boast its chic spa and health bar (features as incongruous in a real 18th-century English country house as a mechanical bull) without raising an eyebrow. Yet reinventions of more recent hotel traditions – the airport hotel, the business hotel and the cheap-but-stylish city centre hotel – can stimulate great design ingenuity, often revealing a shrewd awareness of the perennial value of blending the reassurances of yesterday with the changing tastes of today.

The Ritz-Carlton

Miami, USA 2003

Architects: Nichols Brosch Sandoval & Associates Inc

Interior Design: Howard Design Group

Reinterpreting tradition can often be fraught with dangers – an authentic, original hotel design can all too easily become an empty exercise in style, lacking any real quality beyond that of pastiche. The designers and architects of the newly opened Ritz-Carlton in South Beach, Miami, however, were fortunate enough to be working with a tradition that lent itself particularly well to modern reinvention. The golden age in Miami was the relatively recent 1950s and its signature tradition was a stylish, *moderne* celebration of Floridian seaside leisure. The architect of the original de Lido Hotel, built in 1953, was Morris Lapidus, a Russian émigré whose youthful enthusiasm for theatrical set design eventually evolved into a career designing retail stores and, from the 1940s onwards, hotels and apartments. Miami Beach became Lapidus's professional playground with the de Lido perfectly exemplifying his contribution to a local variant on *Art Moderne*: Miami Modern or Mi-Mo, which was characterized by curves, sweeping lines, pastel accents and joyful motifs.

Architects Nichols Brosch Sandoval & Associates Inc and designers the Howard Design Group have managed to preserve many of the original features of the de Lido Hotel for the Ritz-Carlton makeover. These include the spectacular, black terrazzo floors and a curved wall of polished cherrywood with inlaid and polished, domed light fixtures. If the original *moderne* lines were obliquely inspired by marine imagery, the new design of the 375 guest rooms makes a more overt reference to the staterooms of a luxury liner. Most of them feature colour schemes of nautical blue, spruce green and burnished gold, while the public spaces continue the theme with glass and polished aluminium railings that wind sinuously through the interior. The obligatory European-style quotations include a giant oval rug, with a design based on the metalwork motifs of French *maître ferronier* Gilbert Poillerat, and contemporary Venetian glass chandeliers.

Any modern reinterpretation of a traditional hotel must also find ways of incorporating less traditional but currently fashionable elements into it. The Ritz-Carlton has achieved this by buying into the growing trend for making both art and health facilities part of the hotel offer. Its multi-million dollar art collection shrewdly mixes nostalgia (a recreation of the de Lido's original giant mural) with pastiche (modern artworks from Latin American and European artists 'inspired by the *Art Moderne* era') and prestigious originals (a large Miró etching is proudly displayed in the lower lobby).

RIGHT

The lobby establishes The Ritz-Carlton's curvaceous theme, Miami Modern curves and celebratory motifs. A curved cherrywood wall, studded with domed sconces, draws the visitor through the lobby.

BELOW RIGHT

This archive shot of Lapidus's 1950s design illustrates how the spirit of the original has been retained in the reinterpretation of it.

Incorporated into The Ritz-Carlton is also the La Maîson de Beauté Carita Spa, a 1,486 square metre (16,000 square foot) facility that again revisits the 1950s aesthetic with its stainless steel water wall, Italian mosaic-tiled shallow pool, Venetian stucco walls and – an unusual feature – compressed bamboo floors.

All in all, Nichols Brosch Sandoval & Associates Inc and the Howard Design Group have steered a very astute design course. The half-century that separates Miami traditional from Miami contemporary may only be a relatively brief span of years but public tastes and expectations have changed radically in that period. So, in reviving a recognizable design style without sacrificing either quality or commercial viability, the designers can claim a considerable success here.

ABOVE
Nautical imagery dominates throughout The Ritz-Carlton, with guest rooms that resemble staterooms and external rails that reinforce the idea of being afloat rather than ashore.

RIGHT
This archive shot shows the original hotel entrance, complete with its sinuous logotype and offset guest room windows.

**A hotel surrounded by shades of blue. The Florida sky,
the Atlantic Ocean and the hotel pool combine to give
The Ritz-Carlton in South Beach a luminous setting.**

Four Seasons Hotel

Tokyo, Japan 2002

Architects: Nikken Sekki

Interior Design: Yabu Pushelberg

The extensive Four Seasons family of hotels can fairly claim an established reputation for luxury, if not opulence. Just how far you can push a well-established hotel name, without dislocating its brand perception, has been skilfully demonstrated by George Yabu and Glenn Pushelberg with their interior design of a hotel-within-an-office block. The office block in question, the Pacific Century Palace Tower, is a 31-storey glass building located in Tokyo's dynamic Marunouchi district, a matrix of local transportation, political and commercial energy. It is situated close to Tokyo Station, the Imperial Palace and the Ginza shopping district.

Designed by the Takenaka Corporation (a large Japanese design and build company) with architect Nikken Sekki, the Pacific Century Palace Tower imposed stringent limitations on the hotel that was to be slotted in between its third and seventh floors. These floors had originally been intended for apartments and the conversion to hotel use was only decided on after construction had begun. The challenge for Yabu Pushelberg was to interpret the Four Seasons' traditional brand values and atmosphere in a constrained format that would permit only 57 guest rooms and public areas in an area that could never be described as spacious. They responded to this with a solution that was based not on the familiar scale of a traditional grand hotel, but rather on the model of a private club, where the notion of small, linked salons was not inimical to exclusivity and prestige. Where they encountered a long, narrow rectilinear space the design solution was not to exploit this sudden expanse for its scale but instead to break it up, which resulted in the compact, contiguous spaces of lobby, lounge, bar and restaurant. 'The design is not about one or two grandiose rooms,' notes Glenn Pushelberg, 'but rather about a series of well-executed small spaces that hold together well.'

Other obstacles to overcome included a very mixed array of views, including an unlovely aspect onto the bullet train tracks of the nearby station. Also, the sometimes intrusive monumental structural columns, demanded by law in a country that is prone to earthquakes, posed a challenge of scale in the context of small, salon-like rooms, as did the narrow distance between the guest room windows and the elevator shafts, another legacy of a building primarily designed for offices or apartments. Yabu Pushelberg, however, succeeded in negotiating most of these problems with considerable ingenuity. Elegant translucent screens mask the undesirable views and the huge columns are frequently absorbed into clean, curvilinear walls. As a result of this, each room is largely customized, which has the effect of giving an ongoing variety of experiences to returning guests while affording the designers the flexibility of being able to respond to different spatial challenges and views room by room.

The traditional expectation of a ground-floor lobby with guest rooms above is reversed here, with the rooms located on the four floors below the lobby, bar and restaurant. So what remains of tradition, you may ask? Perhaps it is something in the experience rather than the lineaments. 'This is a modern take on a Japanese *ryokan*' says George Yabu, referring to a traditional type of Japanese inn that has, in recent times, been reinterpreted in many different commercial formats. If the traditional spirit of the *ryokan* was to provide a level of spiritual refuge as well as physical shelter, then perhaps the Four Seasons Tokyo has triumphed in reinventing traditional luxury after all. Even if this tradition is not the familiar Western one, exemplified by the Four Seasons brand, it is still an honourable one that responds to its stringent context with creativity, wit and style.

RIGHT
A bathroom with a view. Blinds provide privacy although the floor-to-ceiling windows do seem to encourage guests to risk charges of exhibitionism while contemplating the vibrant Marunouchi district as they soak in the tub.

LEFT
The entrance to the Pacific Century Palace Tower. Here, the Four Seasons Hotel, a hotel-within-an-office block, is cleverly sandwiched between the third and seventh floors.

LEFT

At times, the contrast in scale between the structural elements of the tower and the hotel's internal spaces cannot be disguised, only minimized by the careful use of colour and finish.

1 TRADITIONAL REINTERPRETATIONS

LEFT

Japan is a country prone to earthquakes so the Pacific Century Palace Tower's massive obligatory supporting columns sometimes had to be carefully camouflaged by the designers.

RIGHT

Yabu Pushelberg's overall approach of linking small public spaces together to suggest an exclusive club finds an echo in the layout of some of the guest rooms.

**Because of the varying
spaces, most rooms in the
Four Seasons Hotel are
customized. This lounge
area features red Zulu hats,
presented as an art piece
on their own table.**

The Grove

Hertfordshire, England, UK 2003

Architects: Fitzroy Robinson; Scott Brownrigg Taylor

Interior Design: Fox Linton Associates; Collett Zarzycki

The Grove, set in 1.2 square kilometres (0.46 square miles) of private parkland, was originally the eighteenth-century Hertfordshire mansion of the Earls of Clarendon. It was built as a country house, a world away from London both in style and distance, but thanks to improved transport links and its proximity to London, it soon became a popular weekend retreat. Two centuries later and it is now hailed as 'London's country estate', where city meets country and classic meets contemporary. The Grove is a bold instance of tradition reinvented, a taste of 18th-century style with added modern convenience.

The task of blending a country setting, an aristocratic history and a sense of metropolitan proximity (London is actually 30 kilometres (18 miles away) fell to Martin Hulbert, Design Director of Fox Linton Associates. Fox Linton had previously enjoyed success with their contribution to One Aldwych, a few years earlier, but here they faced a very different challenge. The original mansion, having been extended several times over the years as the Clarendon family status grew, had acquired another addition. A new west wing had been added to accommodate a new lobby, a restaurant and public rooms for parties, meetings and private entertaining.

All of the hotel's 227 guestrooms and suites have modern facilities including plasma-screen TVs and DVD players The guestrooms in the original mansion are individually designed and retain original architectural features such as open fireplaces. The style cleverly mixes old and new: a giant plasma screen TV may be opposite a Venetian mirror or a piece of contemporary art may hang over an 18th-century chest of drawers. Guestrooms in the West Wing are sleek and contemporary and pursue a slightly different theme, drawing on their proximity to the grounds they overlook. Many open out onto private terraces and Hulbert has cleverly brought the landscape inside by incorporating detailed photographs of leaves onto the Perspex cupboard doors, which are then backlit to dramatic effect.

Presumably this leaf theme does not include any examples of the giant Californian sequoia, although this is the name chosen for the Grove's integrated spa, designed by Collett Zarzycki and featuring twelve treatment rooms, a health bar, two pools (one indoors and mosaic-lined, the other outdoors and sheltered in a walled garden) plus another restaurant – The Stables. Tying many of these style elements together are the public spaces, notably, in the mansion, a series of drawing rooms that lead guests through décor that grades from dark to light, from midnight blues and black to subtle greys and earth tones.

Hulbert claims that many things influenced the overall design of The Grove's new interior: 'The design – especially in the mansion – was influenced by all that is best about a traditional country house: lovely, textured, rich fabrics that wear well; quality furniture; smells from the garden; vases of flowers everywhere and a relaxed welcome.' This fulsome explanation demonstrates that illusion, sensory association and nostalgia play a very real part in many people's view of English traditions. By adding a modern twist to this, Fox Linton have succeeded in creating a contemporary take on country house living.

LEFT
The Grove walks a well-judged line between pastiche and reinvention. Here, the English country garden setting that gives the hotel its unique appeal and atmosphere is visible through the window of this guest room.

RIGHT
The lobby, with its art pieces, eclectic furniture and contemporary reception desk gives early warning that The Grove offers a bracing mix of the old and the new.

LEFT

The staircase is a perfect evocation of the 18th-century country house that is the nucleus of The Grove. The painting, however, confounds any expectations of ersatz family portraits in oils and offers instead a reminder that this particular exercise in traditional reinvention is also a contemporary hotel.

RIGHT

The seahorse detailing of the door handles typifies the attention to detail that characterizes Fox Linton's interior treatment.

LEFT
The 18th-century Hertfordshire mansion in its English country setting, one of the inspirations for the design of The Grove Hotel's interior.

RIGHT
At The Grove, Fox Linton used a design theme that draws on indigenous trees and leaves for inspiration. In the guest rooms, leaf motifs dominate, while in this lounge a wall mirror sprouts branches and flowers.

ABOVE

The detailing in the spa's indoor swimming pool may evoke a traditional English barn, but the ambience has an almost Eastern flavour of calm and retreat.

RIGHT

One of The Grove's more spacious guest rooms in the new contemporary West Wing.

Andél's Hotel

Prague, Czech Republic 2002

Interior Design: Jestico + Whiles

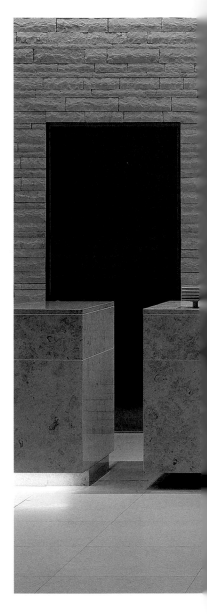

Reinterpreting design traditions in central Europe can pose a particularly demanding and specialized challenge, especially for a foreign designer. Following the fall of the Berlin Wall, Jestico + Whiles were among the first British offices to undertake projects in the former Czechoslovakia as well as in Latvia and Bulgaria. Their first client was the UK Foreign Office and the projects were for cultural and diplomatic premises. The Czech Republic proved particularly amenable to Jestico + Whiles and the company subsequently opened an office in Prague. However, it was their contributions to One Aldwych and The Hempel hotels in London that recommended the firm to clients WARIMPEX and UBM, who appointed them as the interior designers of a new-build hotel that was to form the social focus of Andél City, a new mixed-use Prague development.

Here, unlike their contributions to One Aldwych and The Hempel, Jestico + Whiles were able to execute the whole of the interior design, including the furniture. This holistic approach was to result in a highly coherent design that acknowledged the spirit – and occasionally the letter – of Bohemian craft traditions. The guest's experience of the 280-room hotel begins with a lobby that encourages relaxation rather than the obligatory encounter with the reception desk. The desk itself, offset in its non-confrontational position, is a monolithic block of stone invisibly raised as if it were

hovering above the floor. A decorative theme based on the Bohemian tradition of glass and metal manufacture and sculpture starts here in the lobby. In its central zone a floor-to-ceiling curtain of metallic *voile* defines private and semi-private rooms that are appointed with a writing desk, benches and flower displays behind the shimmering translucent curtain with its echoes of a *shoji* screen. A contemporary reworking of the traditional grand hotel *escalier* features stone steps bordered with etched glass walls, and leads to a first-floor business-guest reception desk, also made of glass. Glass is a reoccurring theme in other public and private spaces in the hotel, including the first-floor restaurant.

The 280 guest rooms maintain a general feel of cool luxury. Materials and the thoughtful use of geometric shapes are the means by which a traditional sense of quality is invoked, without resorting to pastiche. The rooms are flooded with light from the floor-to-ceiling windows, while simple furniture in polished lacquer and glass is designed to allow and indeed encourage guests to adjust its positioning or configuration. There is a movable desk in each room with a rotatable sheet of glass for a top that enables the guest to position and align the piece anywhere in the room. It can be a work desk next to a window or be located beneath a wall-mounted mirror and used as a dressing table. Each room has access to the Internet via Ethernet-LAN and a multimedia TV-System and DVD, and the TV is built into a revolving cube-on-cube, which allows viewing from the bed or from the *chaise longue*. The lower glass-fronted cube houses the minibar while another, separate cube can be used as a footrest, a table or even an extension to the seating area. Instead of using conventional tiles, the bathrooms are lined with full-height sheets of white glass while the lavatory and shower are contained within separate enclosures, defined by frameless glass doors.

The public spaces include a conference suite with a full complement of facilities and a design that again emphasizes flexibility. Sliding panels faced with cream leather can be used to subdivide the space into five smaller rooms within the main space. Taken together, the various spaces within Andél's Hotel fully justify the decision to give one design team the whole remit — instead of competition, there is harmony and consistency. More importantly, instead of a theatrical attempt to revive the past, Jestico + Whiles have found a restrained and contemporary way of effortlessly evoking a certain sense of it.

ABOVE

Andél's monolithic reception desk is given an unexpected touch of visual lightness by being invisibly raised above the reception floor. The vertical stripe in the rectilinear composition hints at the visual manners of Czech Modernism.

LEFT

A contemporary reworking of the traditional grand hotel *escalier* features stone steps flanked by etched glass walls.

BELOW

The Bohemian tradition of decorative glass is referenced in the treatment of the restaurant and throughout the hotel.

LEFT
**The harmony and
consistency that makes
the design work in this
contemporary hotel is
clearly evident in the
main bar.**

34

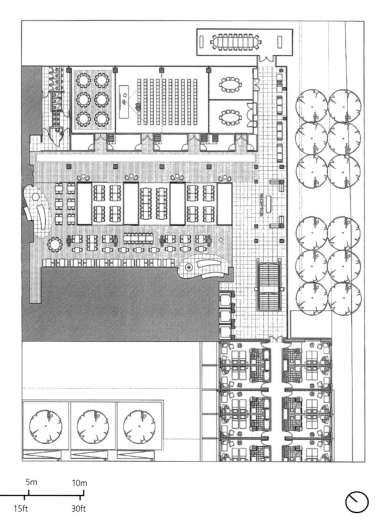

LEFT
The first floor plan.

RIGHT
The health club bar with its icons of human fitness and a light, airy feel.

BELOW
Health club shower cubicles, with their *moiré* enclosures, introduce an ambiguous visual theme combining concealment and transparency.

0   5m   10m

15ft   30ft

The Sheraton Frankfurt Hotel

Frankfurt, Germany 2002

Architects: JSK International

Interior Design: United Designers Europe Ltd

There are traditions and there are traditions. The late 1960s tradition of routinely decking out sternly rectilinear corporate hotels in dull earth tones was one that persisted for a decade and, in places, sometimes much longer. The thinking was transparent (even if the interiors were often contained by glass so densely smoked that it was nearly opaque): make the place look businesslike but use warm tones to replace the utilitarian greys and whites of the office. Passing years and changing tastes have meant that the 'any-colour-so-long-as-it's-brown' solution dated badly and when a hotel designed in this way managed to survive into the present day, it began to look less like a heroic survivor and more like a bad design joke.

The 1,050-room behemoth that is the Sheraton Frankfurt is just such a hotel. It comprises three towers linked by large groundfloor public spaces and a conference centre in the basement. Adjacent to Frankfurt Airport, the hotel has great strategic value but its deeply discouraging design made a radical rethink vital if it was to retain any commercial appeal in the early twenty-first century. United Designers were called in to rework the public areas and 300 executive guest rooms. They were also asked to integrate a new entrance that connected to a railway station providing a new city centre transport link. This new entrance now sets the tone for the hotel and is the guest's first indication that the old Sheraton has discovered a new spectrum of colours, other than brown. A bright blue corridor, 30 metres (98 foot) long, leads from the rail link to a lobby and reception area that has been dramatically reconfigured, having been stripped right back to the building's concrete shell.

The designers were able to create a new set of linked curvilinear spaces that aided orientation and made initial circulation more logical – steel, glass, stone and dark-stained timber are the dominant materials. A central Winter Garden space encloses various activities, giving access to a café, bar and restaurant, entry to the conference centre in the basement and to a viewing area onto the adjacent airport. This linked environment, dedicated to leisure, welcome and meeting places, sets the tone for all the renewed areas in a hotel whose large capacity is an important asset (a sudden influx of delayed air passengers may need to be catered for) but one that is no longer allowed to overwhelm the experience of arrival.

The 300 newly refurbished executive guest rooms are all located in one tower. These rooms continue

the dark-stained wood theme in the furniture, which is upholstered in deep red and mustard fabrics. Stainless steel light fittings and abstract artwork in every room further reflect a more contemporary notion of executive comfort than the old modular beige sofas and biscuit-coloured carpet tiles. The Sheraton Frankfurt Hotel, without rebuilding, has been reinterpreted as much in an architectural sense as through its décor. The strategic use of light to redefine the big spaces, a significant change in circulation and a softening of the old rectilinear lines all combine to change the bone structure of the hotel, making the introduction of a subtle contemporary palette both more logical and more satisfying.

BELOW

The Sheraton Frankfurt Hotel's new bar with its wall of shimmering stainless steel panels.

ABOVE

Visually, the new stair and artwork installation are far removed from The Sheraton Frankfurt's previous design scheme, a 1960s throwback to corporate beige and brown.

LEFT

A stylish reception desk has the physical capacity to accommodate a number of business guests, who may all be checking out at the same time. With its new links to the airport encouraging simultaneous arrivals and departures, this is both an elegant and practical feature.

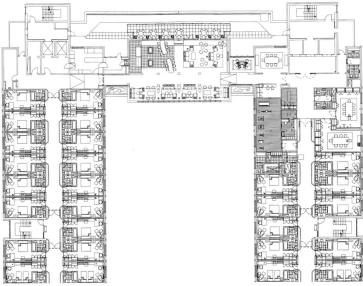

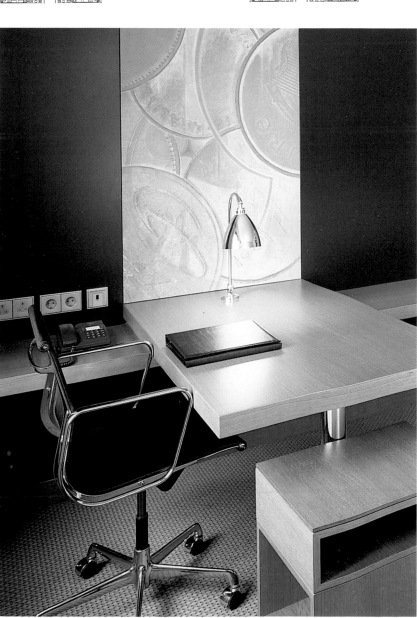

LEFT
A plan showing the ninth floor of the hotel tower – this is the location of the executive rooms that were the first focus of guest room renovation.

RIGHT
The extended lobby introduces natural light into what used to be a smaller space enclosed by smoked glass. This corridor connects the reception area with new transport links.

LEFT
The hotel tower, containing the executive rooms, was the first to be upgraded at The Sheraton Frankfurt. Well-designed and well-appointed work desks form a key feature of each room.

Hart's Hotel

Nottingham, England, UK 2003

Architects: Marsh:Grochowski

Interior Design: Hambleton Decorating Ltd; Stefa Hart

London was not always England's unchallenged style-setter. There was a time when several provincial cities could claim comparable levels of sophistication. However, the city of Nottingham, with a history that evokes mining, D. H. Lawrence, the manufacture of bicycles (Raleigh) and the vague legend of Robin Hood, was rarely seen as being particularly glamorous. The arrival of Hart's Hotel in the centre of the city in 2003 did, though, bring simultaneous touches of class and internationalism to Nottingham and also shook up the traditional concept that people had of a good, small, personal English provincial hotel.

In 1979, Tim Hart had converted a comfortable Victorian house into a country hotel with 15 double bedrooms and a restaurant; this was Hambleton Hall in Rutland, an enduring hotel success story. For his new hotel in Nottingham, Hart commissioned award-winning practice Marsh:Grochowski to build along the exact line of the original Nottingham Castle wall.

'I wanted generous ceiling heights, harmonious proportions in the rooms, and really good ventilation, which would not be mechanical,' says Hart, 'so there are masses of windows you can open.' When the building was complete, Tim Hart handed the interior decoration over to his wife, Stefa, although this was no empty exercise in nepotism. Stefa, daughter of Vladimir Daskaloff who had trained at the Bauhaus, had grown up around the Mediterranean in a world suffused with fine art and the decorative arts. 'Hart's demands simplicity,' Stefa Hart says. 'Painted walls, muted colours, simple curtains, linear furniture – cool, calm and efficient. This is a modern classic hotel that I hope will still look good in 100 years. I am not only a decorator, but also a hotelier – so I am dedicated to making a hotel work, not only visually but in terms of welcome and comfort for the client.' Unsurprisingly contemporary art is a key feature of the principal rooms at the hotel and there is also a collection of abstract pictures painted by Stefa's father.

The bedrooms include furniture by French designer Philippe Hurel, wool carpets in a tufted two-tone stripe made by Gaskell Carpets in Lancashire to Stefa's own design, beds by Beds RZZZZ of Hemel Hempstead and bed linen (goose down pillows and duvets in Egyptian jacquard cotton linen) from Delbanco & Meyer, London. The now obligatory provision of decent electronic amenities in bedrooms here consists of hi-fi and wide-screen TVs and laptop and mobile phone charging facilities; suites include video players and surround sound systems.

Hart's has brought to this busy Midlands town a stylish hotel with good dining and a European sense of luxury. All this has been achieved by an owner whose success was founded in a far more traditional English establishment. The colour and the art, although they might seem naturally at home in many comparable European cities, here represent a particularly bold touch and demonstrate the valuable role a hotel can play in redefining a city's traditional perceptions of itself and even boosting its sense of self-confidence.

RIGHT

Muted colours, linear furniture and a calm atmosphere characterize the Hart's Hotel approach. Designer Stefa Hart has brought something of her love of Bauhaus principles to the public spaces.

LEFT

The hotel entrance signals a particularly European sense of hotel style in a busy Midlands town.

LEFT
Contemporary art is a key feature of the Hart's Hotel interior, including a collection of abstract paintings by Stefa Hart's father, Vladimir Daskaloff.

TOP RIGHT
The European sense of luxury extends to the hotel bar, which is a destination in its own right.

RIGHT
This visually striking solution to the usual stair guardrail uses long, vertical metal strips running the full height of the well.

Hotel Claska

Tokyo, Japan 2003

Architects: Intentionallies; Urban Design Systems Co. Ltd

'The many answers to the question "how to live"'. With this syntactically dubious mission statement, Hotel Claska sets out its ambition to reinvent the very concept of the hotel. Setting aside the idea that even the sort of people who go on *The Jerry Springer Show* to get advice on how to live their lives might think twice before seeking life guidance from a hotelier, Claska is nothing if not original in its thinking.

Its starting point, the eight-storey Hotel New Meguro, was a 35-year-old building located on Tokyo's Meguro Street, a downtown thoroughfare best known for its furniture stores. That hotel stopped trading in 2002 with little prospect of ever reopening since all the prevailing advice suggested that the location (a 3,000-yen/$27) cab ride from the city centre) demanded a budget hotel that simply could not be justified by the amount of investment required to create it. Architecturally speaking, Hotel New Meguro's strange, blocky tile exterior had lost whatever charm it might once have held, and was clearly going to need something both financially and conceptually unusual if it was to be successfully reinvented.

The solution arrived at by client Urban Design Systems Inc was to marginalize the traditional hotel element altogether. This eight-storey building now has just nine guest rooms, which barely qualifies it as a hotel at all. The bulk of the budget was dedicated to the ground-floor lounge space and the fifth and sixth guest room floors. The rest was allocated to a variety of functions, central to which was a 27-room long-stay residential section, providing constant rent in attractive contrast to the variable income from the hotel rooms. Claska's other features reflect the shift of emphasis from traditional hotel to multifunction urban facility, for example, it has no minibars, no gym and no spa. Rather unusually, however, it does have a DJ booth in the middle of the lounge, art galleries, a bookstore and even a grooming centre for dogs.

Intentionallies' 60s/70s-minimalist interiors repeat something of the block-like, rectilinear lines of the original exterior and no two guest rooms are alike. Represented by Tei Shuwa, best known for their cooking appliances, while the contributor of a permanent interactive entrance installation is Steve Baker from the UK outfit Tomato, a firm that trades on an eclectic folio ranging from fashion shows and branding concepts to websites and kiosks. All this reinforces the originality of Urban Design Systems' 'out-of-the-box' thinking, since most firms with an established track record in hotels would invariably have brought along some kind of traditional thinking.

There is, however, nothing traditional about Hotel Claska, which has already become a favourite destination for models, artists and musicians in Tokyo – celebrity DJs have even been known to come down from their guest rooms for a session in the lobby DJ booth. The overall lesson seems to be that the hotel dimension now exists less to make money in its own right than to help to position Claska as a fashionable, transient urban centre, a club where trendy things happen in an atmosphere that encourages passing through, whether for an hour, a week or a month.

BELOW

Hotel Claska, the former Hotel New Meguro, still exemplifies an arresting brand of 60s brutalism on Tokyo's downtown Meguro Street.

RIGHT

A bookshop is just one diverse purpose to which the complex housing Hotel Claska now lends itself.

‹503
504
505
506

501›
502

PREVIOUS PAGES
The heavy, blocky lineaments of the original building are celebrated in Intentionallies' unique 60s/70s-minimalist interior treatment.

ABOVE AND RIGHT
Hotel Claska's eight-storey building houses just nine hotel guest rooms. The rest of the building is allocated to a variety of functions including long-stay rooms and suites.

FAR RIGHT
The entrance to Claska's dog grooming facility, complete with symbolic kennels – an idiosyncratic addition to this bright-and-buzzy, multifunction, urban 'socialspace'.

Ku'Damm 101

Berlin, Germany 2003

Architects: Eyl, Weitz, Würmle & Partner

Design and Concept: kessler und kessler

Once there was a recognizable hierarchy of hotels in which stars, rosettes or other such awards reliably indicated certain standards; below this came the more modest establishments, bed-and-breakfasts, guest houses and so on. These latter categories rarely attempted to entertain guests or offer more than basic food and accommodation. Today, the old distinctions are rapidly being eroded making hotels like Ku'Damm 101 much harder to pigeon-hole. Technically it is a three-star hotel, but then so are hundreds of other, much duller places. Ku'Damm 101 is a clever adaptation of a nondescript office block on Berlin's famous shopping street. Named after the building number and street it is situated on, this hotel's ambitions, expressed by kessler und kessler's efficient design, involve comfort, practicality and minimalism.

If the hotel has a sense of luxury, it is achieved not by trying for a cut-price version of expensive effects but by suggesting excellence through discreet taste and by making the practical things – mattresses, worktables, flooring – of the highest quality. The result is a cool, lifestyle hotel that, by being close to Berlin's trade fair centre, primarily targets the business traveller. However, it also appeals to short-stay tourists and those who appreciate a confident style of German design that embraces Le Corbusier's theories on colour (a restrained palette of greys, blues, greens and mauves) and a redefinition of luxury in terms of reduction to the pure and simple. Even the logo shows a certain minimalist bravado, consisting only of a stylized apostrophe that has been taken from the hotel name: a typographical symbol that indicates something has been omitted is satisfyingly appropriate in a hotel that consciously omits Grand Hotel effects in favour of something more economical.

The adoption of Le Corbusier's colour theories is not an idle affectation: kessler und kessler took care to acquire the pigments from a Swiss company that still produces them to the original guidelines of the architect, who believed that colour could compensate for missing architecture. Colour can also minimize the negative effects of unwanted architecture as kessler

und kessler demonstrated when disguising some of the exposed structural elements from the former office building. The lobby floor consists of natural asphalt, a surface that is intended to acquire an attractive patina of wear over time. The vertical surfaces, including the check-in desk, are faced with American walnut.

The design approach taken in the 170 guest rooms was essentially a reductive one, providing only a bed, a table, a chair and a closet, all designed by Munich's Lemongras (*sic*) Design Studio. The table tops, however, were made to be adaptable in size, doubling as writing desks or dining tables; the closets are large enough to accommodate a range of different clothing and the rooms themselves are all spacious enough to take an extra bed if needed. In this rigorous context, the decision to wrap the curvy TV cabinet in retro zebrano veneer looks almost wildly decadent but even this playful unit is highly functional, incorporating an Internet terminal fed by wireless LAN (Local Area Network) throughout the hotel. This pioneering touch is, strangely enough, often only available in budget hotels and not the more luxurious ones but it is one service that will surely be universal in a few years.

There were conscious decisions not to install mini-bars in the guest rooms, not to provide room service and – in what may soon prove to be an exceptional point of distinction in a world where hotel spas seem to be obligatory – no dedicated fitness or health facilities. Instead, guests have access to vending machines, a lobby bar that doubles as a take-out restaurant, a supermarket within the hotel and the option to hire a stocked mini-refrigerator. Working off the calories can be done with hired exercise equipment that is intended to be used in the privacy of the guest's room.

Ultimately, the Ku'Damm is an unusual but successful venture that may well point the way for many other urban hotels in the twenty-first century. The design effects used here have been achieved by creating attractive facilities and finishes that are appropriate to today's business traveller and style-conscious tourist and not by rolling out some cheap pastiche of a previous century's concept of luxury.

RIGHT

Ku'Damm 101's bid to suggest quality through good taste, rather than expensive materials, is reflected in its lobby where colour and form combine to create a distinctive atmosphere. The unashamed disguising of massive structural columns makes a virtue out of a necessity.

The dining room, with its prominent hotel name signature on the wall and one of its ubiquitous supporting columns unavoidably accommodated by the space and the colour scheme.

Ku'Damm's bold use of colour extends to the guest rooms, adding a sense of enjoyment that does not depend upon expense.

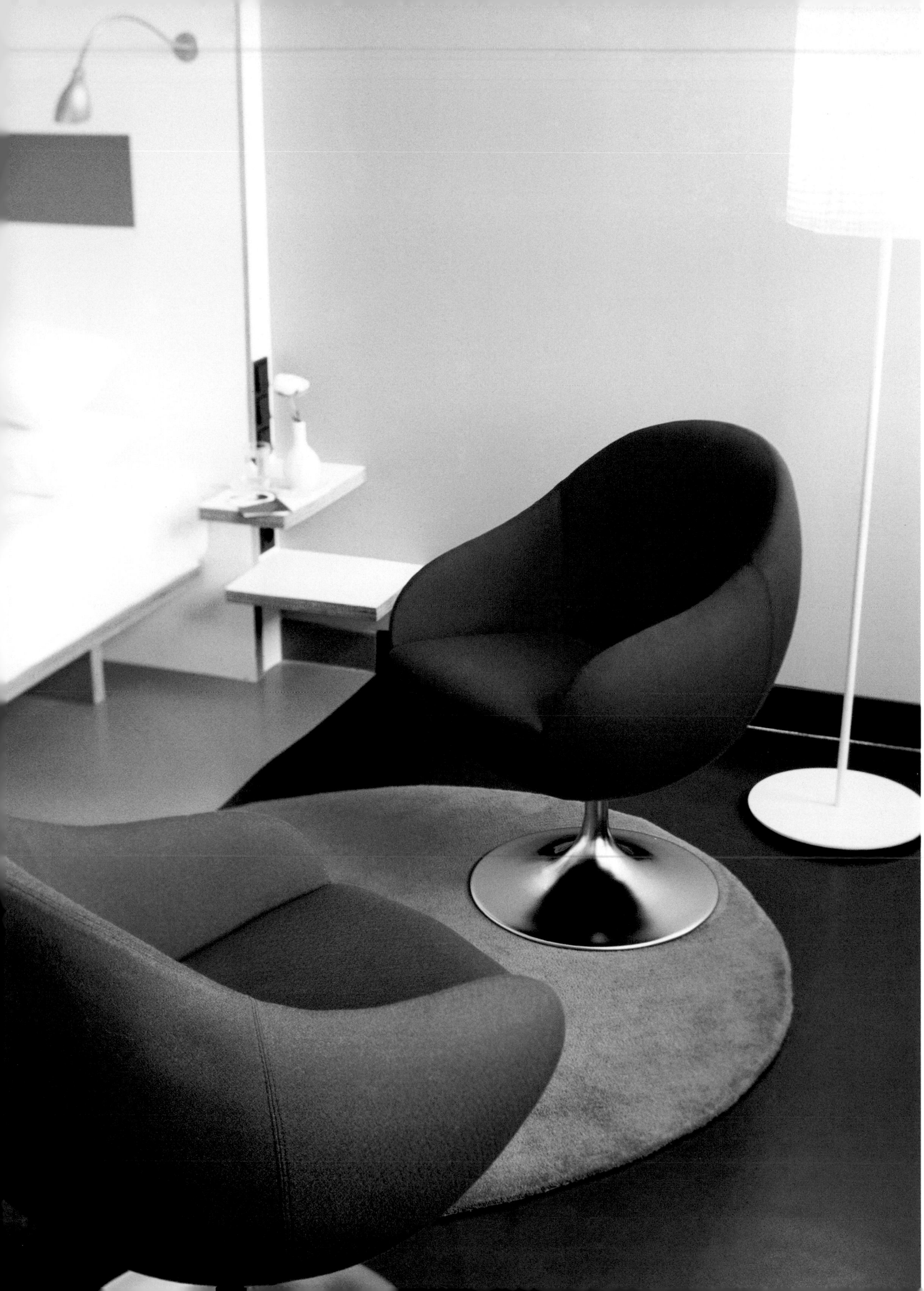

The check-in desk, like most of the vertical surfaces in the lobby, is faced with American walnut. The lobby floor, meanwhile, uses natural asphalt, an inexpensive and easy to maintain surface that acquires an attractive patina of wear over time.

LEFT

Making a virtue out of a simple finish, this sink and shower area has overtones of institutional tiling but remains perfectly attractive and unfussy in Ku'Damm's calculated context of good quality minimalism.

LEFT

Despite a cluster of supporting columns in this example of one of the hotel's 170 guest rooms, the overall image is one of space and light. The furniture, by Lemongras Design Studio, includes a sinuous TV cabinet in zebrano veneer.

1 TRADITIONAL REINTERPRETATIONS

25hours Hotel

Hamburg, Gemany 2003

Interior Architect: Evi Maeklstetter

Interior Design: Armin Fischer

25hours Hotel is designed by 3Meta Maerklstetter + Fischer and marketed by design hotels™ as 'an answer to the lifestyles of creative, metropolitan nomads'. The metropolitan nomads in question are not, as the phrase may suggest, vagrants that are forever being moved on by the police, dragging their creative cardboard box homes behind them, but young movers and shakers from the media world. At least this is what the reception desk of this new Hamburg hotel strongly indicates. Studded with 420 convex mirrors and hovering above a plush pink carpet and a glowing band of light, suggestive of imminent take-off, the desk is an early indication that 25hours Hotel is neither a quiet refuge nor an oasis of calm in a busy city. Spilling out from the ceiling, two six-metre (20-foot) circles of light create a continuum of projected colours that changes the ambiance of the reception area, that is artfully dotted about with stools in leather and pink fabric, throughout the day.

As visitors negotiate all of this on their way to the lifts, they are confronted with another bank of mirrors, this time gimbal-mounted to multiply and reflect the lobby from a variety of different angles. 'As soon as guests step out of the lift, these mirrors show them exactly who and what is going on in the lobby,' says 3Meta principal Armin Fischer, sounding more like a security guard than a designer. Not so, it seems: 'The lobby of 25hours Hotel is all about seeing and being seen,' he explains. Exactly how one is seen rather depends on the time of day since those ceiling-mounted, ambiance-changing lights favour clear, bright colours for the ante-meridian hours ('to wake up and energize') and a whole range of lively hues working their way towards a synthetic sunset of 'red and pink club lighting' in the evening.

The pivoting mirrors mark the start of an area, called The Event Area. This 320 square metre (3,444 square foot) space, with a large open fire as its main feature, is designed to accommodate special events and meetings. The area also doubles as a lounge with sofas, stools and quadrant tables that are all easily movable, making it easy to reconfigure the space into various modules when necessary. On the third floor is The Living Room, which takes the form of another lounge roughly half the size of The Event Area. It is aimed at giving overnight guests a kind of common room or den to relax and play in. Table soccer and video screenings are available, but it also acts as a meeting place for youthful media types who, it is

thought, thrive on meetings and social get-togethers. Vending machines, cups and glasses are kept here with the idea of providing a more informal kind of community room with grey sofas and a six metre (20 foot) zebrano wood table as the main furniture.

The hotel's 65 guest rooms continue the theme of 'style without luxury' with their cheerful retro mix of pseudo 60s lines and contemporary colours. The base colours are pastel blues and greens but, throughout, white predominates. Most of the furniture was designed specifically for 25hours Hotel by the 3Meta design team who clearly have a liking for the sort of rounded-corner lines that Macintosh computers favoured at the start of the twenty-first century. A white, multi-purpose table can be used as seating, a writing desk or a suitcase rack and a pastiche 60s lamp, Spun1 by Sebastian Wrong for Flos, was initially produced expressly for 25hours Hotel.

The lamp, like most of the rest of the furnishing, can be purchased or ordered from reception, as can goody bags containing the sort of things some hotels offer gratis: for example, toiletries – its 'Hangover Package – For The Day After' is perhaps rather revealing. Here, in fact, lies the essence of 25hours Hotel. At its heart it is a budget hotel but it places the emphasis on fashion, style, trends and what it hopes is a young ambiance. It seems to be less a fashionable watering hole for moneyed media professionals than a relentlessly energetic, souped-up hostel for younger media people who were perhaps students not all that long ago.

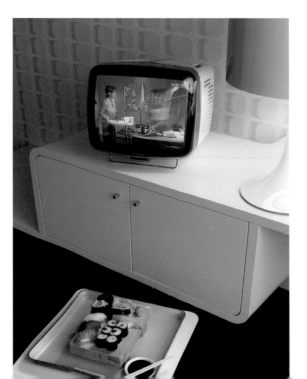

LEFT
Simply appointed rooms send out a message of 'style without luxury' using a cheerful retro mix of 60s lines and pastel colours. Most of the furniture was specifically designed by the 3Meta team who favour a soft, rounded-corner look.

In the lobby two six-metre (20-foot) circles of light are projected from the ceiling. The colours change throughout the day to create shifting moods and atmosphere.

A bank of swivel-mounted convex mirrors multiply and reflect the lobby from a variety of different angles.

ABOVE
A public bathroom continues the 25hours theme of bold colour, light washes and dramatic shapes. It also features a video screen.

LEFT
Public seating in a lobby where everyone is clearly on display.

RIGHT
More atmospheric lighting in the hotel lounge, complete with log store and expansive sofas.

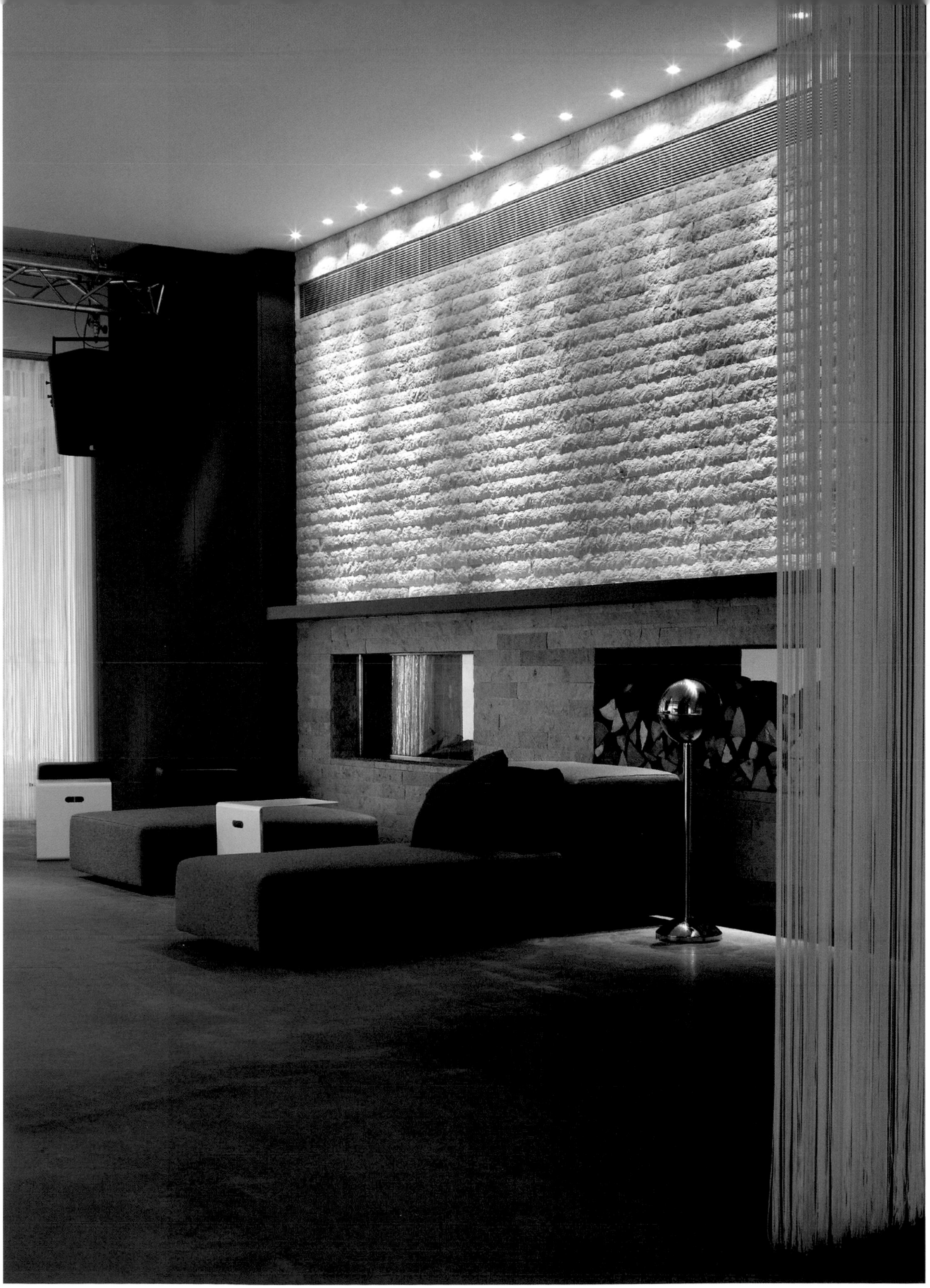

2 Mainstream Experiments

In between the wilder shores of designer hotels and careful attempts to reinterpret the traditional hotel, lies the world of mainstream hotels. Mainstream does not necessarily mean bland, although creating experimental design treatments for hotel chains can prove a stiff challenge. Many such chains have difficulty letting go of corporate concepts such as using a pan-global design treatment for guest rooms, which means that waking up in one of their hotel rooms in Amsterdam is indistinguishable from waking up in one in Tokyo. W Hotels, however, have taken what would once have been called designer hotels into the mainstream – their international city hotels are now characterized by a design-led approach rather than any one-design style. In the UK, the myhotel group has also given notice of its commitment to incorporate a sense of fun and fashionability into an accessible hotel chain, while Apex is building a reputation for making its business hotels also attractive enough for a family break. To set the seal on this acceptance of imaginative design into the mainstream, radical designers Yabu Pushelberg were even given an almost free rein at a Le Meridien hotel in the heart of the American Midwest.

myhotel Chelsea

London, England, UK 2002

Architects and Interior Design: Project Orange

It is arguable whether the myhotel concept should properly be considered to be a mainstream experiment rather than a variant type of designer hotel. However, the case for treating it as nouveau mainstream hinges on the way that individual myhotels respond to, reinforce and reflect back the character of the locale they are in. This, after all, is what the best mainstream hotels used to do so effortlessly in the days before the big brand chains moved in and imposed their standardized hospitality experience, regardless of context or neighbourhood.

Andy Thrasyvoulou's burgeoning myhotel concept demonstrates that he too is obsessed with brands, although not necessarily his own. Borrowed themes and slogans are deployed to glamorize the spirit of a particular myhotel according to its setting. myhotel Brighton will be 'Maharishi Meets Freddie Mercury' claims Thrasyvoulou, as if such a meeting might actually be a good thing! The theme for myhotel Paddington, which is situated near a major London rail terminal, will be 'Where Travel Meets Time', while the recently completed myhotel Chelsea is characterized as a union between *Brideshead Revisited* and *Sex and the City*. If this is all reminiscent of a rather desperate Hollywood movie pitch ('It's *Out of Africa* meets *Pretty Woman*,' says a hopeful script agent at the start of Robert Altman's film, *The Player*) it does identify a keen awareness of the contemporary power of brands and lifestyle associations in the context of hotel design.

Apart from its unique 'theme', myhotel Chelsea also trades on its chic address and its proximity to a number of stylish stores, restaurants and boutiques. Out of a conventional hotel building, designer James Soane of Project Orange has created an ersatz English country home into which American *feng shui* practitioner, William Spear, has injected the kind of furniture placements that, in reality, would rarely preoccupy the owners of a real English country home. Forty-five bedrooms, studios and suites similarly combine the old with the new, using pastel décor, eclectic furniture (an unashamed marriage of antique and contemporary) and the mandatory flat screen TVs, DVD and CD players plus Internet access. The Thai Suite is a reinvention of an earlier luxury facility that was already present in the original hotel, before myhotel moved in, and similarly mixes the traditional with the modish.

Two delinquent bedrooms, located behind the bar, are explicitly designed to accommodate the kind of spontaneous sexual encounters that require inflammatory decor and access to a serious supply of alcohol. Ruby and Scarlet, as these rooms are archly labelled, feature hot reds and pinks, 'polar bear' throws, erotic photographs and low light levels. The advertised opportunity to book either room at short notice with the bartender on duty gives more than a suggestion of where the *Sex and the City* tag comes in, even if the stately decadence of *Brideshead Revisited* remains rather more elusive. myhotel Chelsea, though, sells itself primarily through its service. It is a 'personalized' hotel in which a menu of individual preferences (form to be filled in prior to arrival) is combined with nostalgic gimmicks, such as summertime ice-cream van chimes and afternoon tea with a bone china service, alongside the obligatory health facility and a restful conservatory ('in which residents can escape,' says the hotel blurb, perhaps unwisely).

The décor throughout this hotel is essentially a stage set, a backdrop to a theatrical smorgasbord of New Age guest experiences, zestfully themed on how mainstream English hotels might look if only all mainstream locations were like Chelsea.

RIGHT

Where *Brideshead Revisited* meets *Sex and the City*; myhotel Chelsea is not afraid to pitch itself as a feel-good experience as this promotional shot of a guest room and the lower half of a guest indicates.

ABOVE
Pastel décor, an eclectic mix of furniture and input from a *feng shui* expert combine to make myhotel's guest rooms a more sensual experience than most.

RIGHT
Even the corridors at myhotel Chelsea are infused with a sense of drama and expectation.

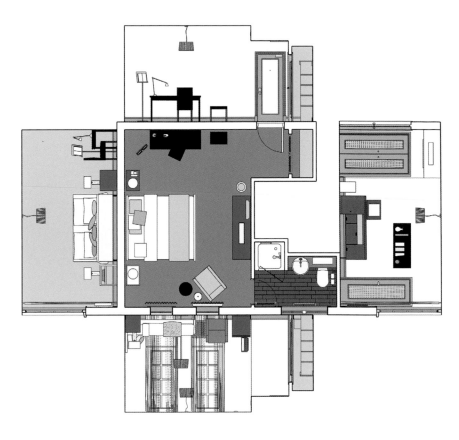

ABOVE

A clever fold-out plan of one of the guest rooms at myhotel in Chelsea. London.

RIGHT

The conservatory comes into its own in the summer, bringing a hint of the traditional country house to what is in fact an ultra-urban chic hotel.

ABOVE

The public spaces incorporate something of the feel of a stage set with all the flattering implications of making guests feel like performers with a role to play.

W Mexico City

Mexico City, Mexico 2003

Architects: KMD

Interior Design: Studio GAIA

The W brand, owned by Starwood Hotels & Resorts Worldwide Inc, represents an ongoing attempt to create an international chain of hotels where the unifying factor is not a uniformly applied visual style but rather a consistent preoccupation with a dynamic idea of 'style', to be interpreted in different ways at different locations. In 2003, the eighteenth W property, W Mexico City, was launched. Starwood jointly developed this 25-storey, 237-room hotel with the Mexico City-based Grupo Plan SA de CV, employing the New York design team Studio GAIA to impart the latest W look.

Architecturally eye-catching, the KMD-designed hotel building stakes its claim in the sophisticated Polanco neighbourhood of Mexico City with an all-glass façade that turns the hotel into a sophisticated goldfish bowl for passers-by. The image is a felicitous one, since the series of stepped lounge areas in the lobby appear to float on water, with various koi ponds visible beneath the walkways and seating areas. A black lava stone tunnel leads to the hotel reception, while bars and restaurants are accessed by negotiating a series of loosely connected 'islands' of seating, upholstered in white leather and yellow fabric. These rise in a spiral formation to The Whiskey, Rande Gerber's first bar outside the US, and one of the premium attractions of the hotel. Another focus is the second-floor restaurant, Solea, developed by Cornerstone, the outfit that was responsible for Chicago's one sixtyblue and Wave restaurants.

The enclosed glass theme is extended through to the hotel spa, with its centrepiece sauna based not on Scandinavian pine but the traditional Mexican adobe hut. The whole spa is surrounded by green glass, as is the health club workout room that overlooks – and is overlooked by – the street. The guestrooms also challenge conventional notions – cherry red ceilings and white terrazzo floors invert the usual tonal arrangement, while the bathrooms have been promoted into major spaces in their own right. Covered in light-hued stone, the over-sized bathrooms feature window views, large 'rain'-style showers with additional body jets and even optional hammocks.

W Mexico City has a full-service business centre, including meeting facilities and a conference centre, and it also offers a special programme to ease its business guests 'into a creative frame of mind with lively music, smells, tastes and visuals'. At this kind of level, the hospitality sounds not just comprehensive but relentless, perhaps catering more towards the more adventurous type of guest. Such a guest, having emerged from The Whiskey bar and successfully negotiated its spiral access trail without falling into a koi pond, would seem to crave a doze in a wet hammock before working out in the full gaze of pedestrians strolling by in the city's famously polluted air. No doubt in practise the experience is far more relaxed, although as Barry S. Sternlicht, Chairman and CEO of Starwood Hotels points out, 'This is certainly our most avant-garde hotel yet'. He adds, 'The design is sophisticated, vibrant, sexy and full of surprises – which fits in well with Mexico City, and particularly the Polanco neighbourhood.'

ABOVE
The 25-storey W Mexico City is a conventional tower block with some very unconventional public spaces within.

LEFT
The hotel spa is surrounded by green glass, as is the health club workout room that overlooks the street.

RIGHT
The dining area extends the hotel's theme of a glass envelope that encourages clear views out of and into the building.

Local ethnic touches in the form of a warm, adobe-inspired colour scheme and a variety of simulated tree trunks in a public space off the main lobby.

A guest room with a glimpse into one of the bathrooms where 'rain-type' shower systems and removable hammocks add a touch of the exotic and even the unexpected.

W New York – Times Square

New York, USA 2002

Architects: Brennan Beer Gorman Architects

Interior Design: Yabu Pushelberg

The real estate site of W New York – Times Square was originally intended to be the home of a Planet Hollywood hotel before the whole Planet Hollywood enterprise ran into financial difficulties during its construction. Instead, the site went to Starwood Hotels & Resorts Worldwide Inc who recruited the ascendant Toronto-based firm of Yabu Pushelberg. They were to carry on the tradition of design-aware W hotels that was first established in 1998 in Manhattan with the W hotel at 49th Street and Lexington Avenue. The W New York – Times Square was the sixteenth in the W chain to open worldwide and posed a particular challenge for Yabu Pushelberg, if only because of the raucous nature of its locale – only in such a hyperactive urban context could a building as gargantuan as the nearby Marriott Marquis actually get lost in the landscape.

Yabu Pushelberg's solution was typical of their usual approach, briskly characterized as 'class for the mass' by Glenn Pushelberg. They created a serene internal landscape that seems to float above the kerbside hustle from which the transitional entrance area provides an immediate refuge, with a cascading glass-enclosed water wall accompanied by the sound of crashing waves from above.

Beyond this aquatic introduction, the reception lounge and lobby quickly establishes a human scale with a mix of private booths made of resin and low communal seating for larger groups. A backlit resin table top bar with ash stain wood finish adds a touch of the class for what Pushelberg likes to call the mass, and the overall feel is one of an accessible, good quality environment, removed from (but still connected to) the febrile atmosphere of one of the world's most famous intersections.

The neutral coloured guest rooms are painted in textured grey and feature more of the omnipresent resin fixtures that Yabu Pushelberg have used liberally throughout the hotel; here they encase the mini-bar and TV, suggesting design-awareness without overstating it in what is essentially a contemporary look that does not want to appear too trendy.

If the W New York – Times Square has a stand-out focal point, there is no mistaking exactly what it is: The Blue Fin Restaurant. The restaurant contract had already been given to Steve Hanson, whose previous concept restaurants (Fiamma, The Blue Water Grill and Ruby Foo's) had firmly established him on the New York dining scene, when Yabu Pushelberg were brought on board. Hanson was not initially impressed, being

used to having more design control, but the Canadian designers eventually won him round with an extension of the entrance theme. They devised a romantic, undulating marine-inspired treatment, featuring a plaster wall that mimics ribbed sand, a starfish wall and a fish mobile by Japanese artist Hirotoshi Sawada. The two-level restaurant's entrance is through a 'storefront' bar with large windows that face onto Broadway. Illuminated resin bar tables – apart from prompting the thought that Yabu Pushelberg must have negotiated a really great deal with their resin supplier – act as beacons for the passing public.

Throughout the restaurant's two levels are a series of smaller spaces that seek to introduce an intermittent sense of intimacy, in what is in fact quite a large 400-seater establishment. The restaurant's lower level has a faster feel and look, more attuned to the energy levels of the street, while the upper section subtly uses colour and texture to achieve a more subdued and reflective atmosphere. The Blue Fin is the destination element within the W New York – Times Square, which has now become a target for New York visitors who want a touch of class without the overwhelming sense of participating in a full-blown designer hotel experience.

BELOW

The hotel bar with a backlit display of bottles – drinking and dining are the focus of this very public hotel that faces both onto Broadway and Times Square.

RIGHT

One of several marine references in the hotel, all of which have been inspired by The Blue Fin restaurant. This mobile by Hirotoshi Sawada above the main stairs evokes a shoal of fish swimming individually but in concert.

LEFT
Large, square tables with circular stools are complemented by contemporary lighting.

PREVIOUS PAGE LEFT
A luminous art piece hovers aloft in a secluded section of The Blue Fin restaurant.

PREVIOUS PAGE RIGHT
A restrained guest room in a hotel located near one of the least restrained intersections in Manhattan, outside can be seen a night view of Times Square and the city.

The dune-ribbed pattern of The Blue Fin restaurant makes a spectacular introduction to Steve Hanson's hip eaterie. Other Hanson restaurants in New York include Fiamma and The Blue Water Grill.

BELOW

These glowing resin bar tables are conspicuously displayed near the windows that face onto Broadway, so attracting passing trade as well as servicing the needs of hotel guests.

W New York – Union Square

New York, USA 2000

Architects: Brennan Beer Gorman Architects

Interior Design: The Rockwell Group

The Rockwell Group is a design firm that has made a name for itself with a wide range of outstanding leisure and recreation facilities as well as residential and business premises. Casinos, restaurants, sports architecture, bars and clubs all reflect principal David Rockwell's fascination with theatre in all its varied forms. The firm's headquarters are in Union Square, Manhattan, which, coincidentally, was also the site of a fine old insurance company building that was to become the second New York W hotel to be built by Starwood Hotels & Resorts Worldwide Inc in 2000.

Unlike Times Square, Union Square has enjoyed an uneven role and reputation over the years. Once the focal point of an elegant area, today Union Square is an undistinguished park, the site of an occasional produce market and a place that is seemingly forever undergoing some kind of slow and inconclusive renovation. Union Square is also the lower mid-town location of a major subway interchange station and remains a site that is still lacking in any distinctive characteristics, although it does boast several surrounding buildings of merit. One such building is the Guardian Life Building on Park Avenue South; built in 1911, with additions in the 1960s, it is, without doubt, one of the best in the area.

This 20-storey granite and limestone landmark structure with its famous four-storey mansard roof was re-imagined by The Rockwell Group and architect of record Brennan Beer Gorman Architects as an extension of Union Square Park. The lobby acts as a kind of living room, looking out onto the grassy public space to which the building is notionally attached with the use of planted grass. The gracious living of an earlier age was evoked for this W hotel, mainly through a newly built grand staircase of limestone, mahogany and steel that rises dramatically from the ground floor to a ballroom on the next level. Coffered ceilings and vaulted marble hallways add further suggestions of the elegance of the past. If this is hotel décor as theatre, however, it is theatre of a restrained sort and some way removed from earlier Rockwell pastiches like the oriental restaurant, Ruby Foo's. This project was self-confessedly based not upon original Asian styles and materials but on the particular look of a minor 1960 movie, *The World of Suzy Wong*. Despite this, playful touches and quotations are still to found at the W and were apparently inspired by the Green Market, a local produce fair that sets up its stalls on certain days of the week in the park. A small lawn of green grass sits unexpectedly on top of the reception desk and boxes of the same grass flank the staircase. Giant wall panels, made of richly-grained makore wood, feature mother-of-pearl buttons and elsewhere, in the living room-cum-lobby, real ivy plants hang from the walls, while spotlights project a yellow flower-petal pattern onto the ceiling.

If the hope is to echo something of the design elements from early 20th-century parks and gardens, then the danger is that the real park outside rather undercuts this aspiration; to date, the internal public spaces of the W New York – Union Square certainly look more verdant and well tended than the rather run-down external public space of the actual square. The 270 guest rooms, however, do not continue with the theme of plants and foliage, being cosy and whimsical only insofar as the beds are covered in shiny sharkskin covers and appointed with leather headboards. Otherwise, they employ a natural palette of aubergine, taupe and browns and generally adhere to restrained contemporary lines.

RIGHT

Le Grand Escalier reinvented. This impressive limestone, mahogany and steel staircase rises from the hotel lobby to a ballroom on the next floor. It succeeds in evoking the former grandeur of the old building while adding playful details such as the grass plantings.

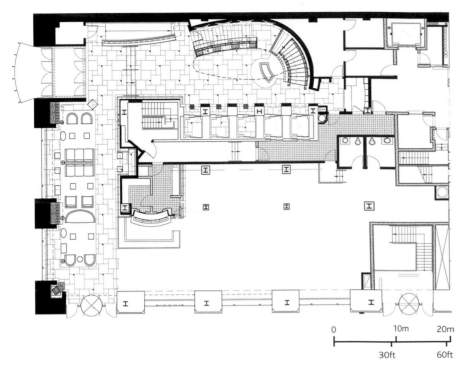

LEFT
A plan of the hotel's ground floor.

0   10m   20m

30ft   60ft

LEFT
Subtle floral motifs line the illuminated wall recesses and lend extra drama and an enhanced sense of height to the hotel's signature staircase.

RIGHT
Indoor topiary at the W New York – Union Square. A recurring motif, a yellow flower, is used to decorate the recessed objects.

RIGHT
This part of the lobby adopts the visual manners of a well-appointed living room, its comfortable atmosphere contrasting with the metropolitan view and the surrounding scale of a distinguished civic building.

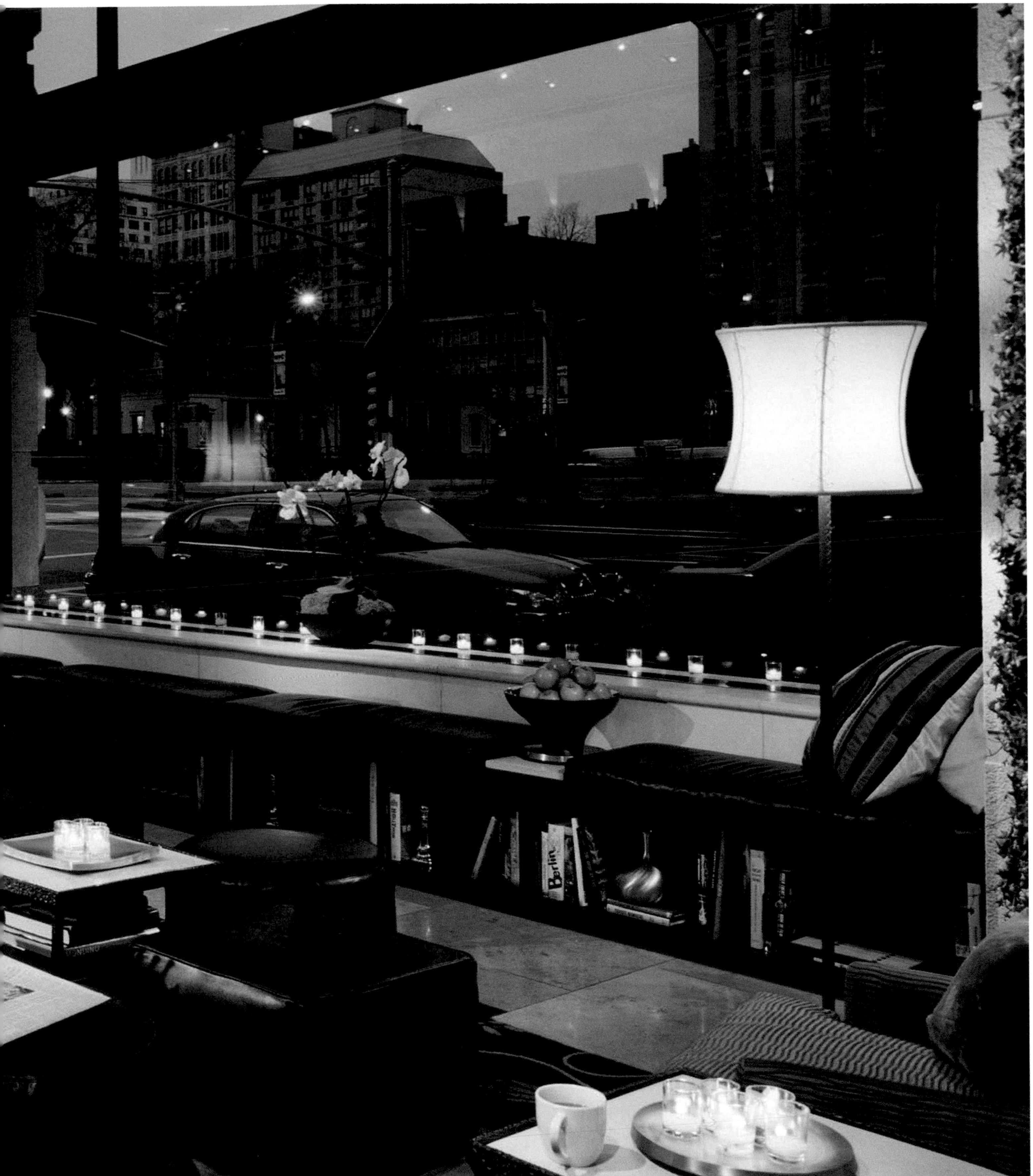
Berlin

Apex City Hotel

Edinburgh, Scotland, UK 2002

Architects and Interior Design: Ian Springford Architects

In recent times, Edinburgh has had cause to adapt a number of its grand old buildings to contemporary purposes. However, the starting point for Ian Springford Architects' hotel conversion of The Bank of Scotland offices in the city's Grassmarket district was neither particularly grand nor old; it was a mid-1970s structure that posed a number of more recent design challenges.

The brief was to create a four-star hotel in a small, central district lying just to the south of Castle Rock, an important focal point of the Old Town since at least the fifteenth century. Before design work could get underway, some setbacks concomitant with the original building's time of construction were encountered. The discovery of asbestos was found to be more extensive than was originally estimated and the concrete waffle slab construction imposed some restrictions on where it could be penetrated to accommodate services and the positioning of bathrooms. In the end, the existing building services were completely stripped out and replaced with a new configuration to accommodate the large mechanical air-handling plant that ventilates the bar, restaurant and kitchen as well as plumbing and sanitary services for the en suite bathrooms and structured cabling for in-room entertainment systems, ISDN and other telecommunications equipment. Such 'invisible' challenges and tasks are real enough to complicate any adaptive design scheme. They offer a reminder that architectural conversion usually involves considerably more than simply overlaying an imaginative new scheme onto the bones of an old structure.

Once the initial practical difficulties had been overcome, Ian Springford Architects chose to remove a section of the existing building on the Grassmarket elevation and insert a glazed tower and canopy in its place. This allowed for the creation of semi-public library spaces for guests to relax outside their rooms in a location overlooking the famous castle. The rear of the building was also removed in order to open up the building for an extension that permitted the creation of larger bedrooms. These bedrooms were designed with different zones for working, sleeping and relaxing. The finish of the floor, grading from timber to carpet, differentiates the areas. Larger than average bathrooms are generally a feature of Apex hotels and at Apex City Hotel porcelain mosaic floor tiles, white glazed wall tiles, limestone vanity tops and cherrywood veneer have been used to enhance the spatial impact of a walk-in shower and separate bath.

One of the benefits of the reconfiguration of this ex-office building was that an unusually long restaurant with direct access from the street was achievable.

BELOW RIGHT
An elegant conclusion to an exceptionally challenging architectural task, converting the original building involved stripping out the original building services and working within the spatial limitations of a 1970s concrete waffle-slab construction.

The public areas use a restrained palette of materials, featuring limestone-finished floors and walls in the entrance, lobby and libraries. Restaurant and bar areas are lined with American black walnut slats, which follow the distinctive curved corners that defined the original building, and the bar is clad in black limestone with integrated ice wells for displaying seafood and champagne. A back bar features Swiss pear timber-veneered glass panels that are backlit to illuminate an impressive display of whiskies in a room that is furnished in dark grey suede.

Apex has three other hotels in the region – another in Grassmarket, the Apex European elsewhere in Edinburgh and the Apex City Quay Hotel and Spa in Dundee – and now plans to open another hotel, this time in London. This expansion of Apex Hotels is testimony to a successful relationship with Ian Springford Architects, whose approach to adapting a variety of buildings into superior mainstream hotels suggests that they have been unusually successful in combining adaptive architectural skills with imaginative interior design.

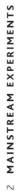

2 MAINSTREAM EXPERIMENTS

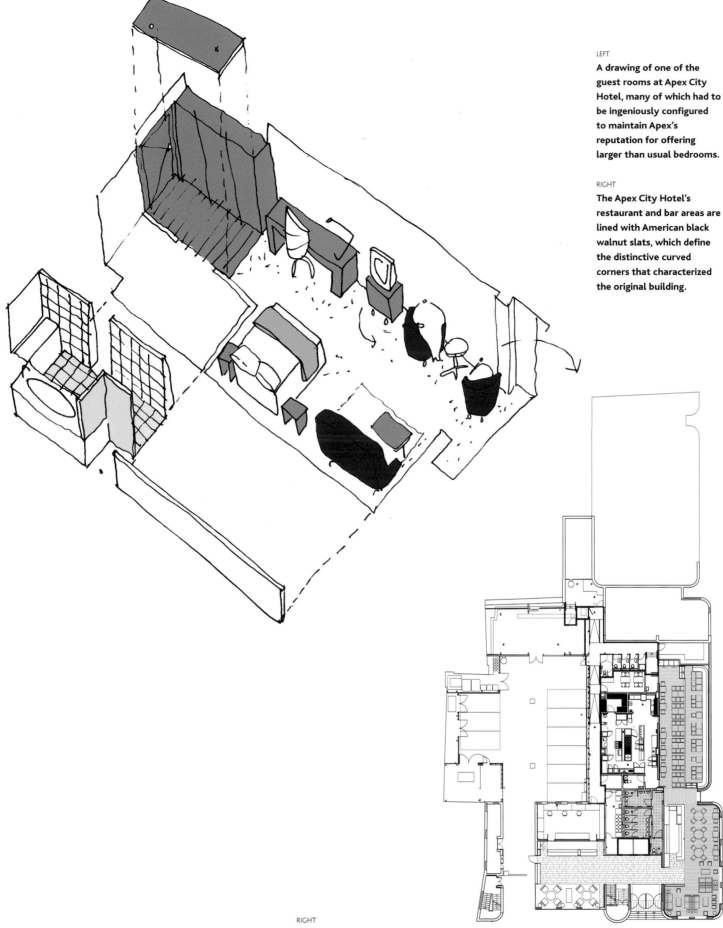

A floor plan of the hotel.

LEFT

A drawing of one of the guest rooms at Apex City Hotel, many of which had to be ingeniously configured to maintain Apex's reputation for offering larger than usual bedrooms.

RIGHT

The Apex City Hotel's restaurant and bar areas are lined with American black walnut slats, which define the distinctive curved corners that characterized the original building.

2 MAINSTREAM EXPERIMENTS

Malmaison

Birmingham, England, UK 2003

Architects: Ferrier Crawford

Interior Design: Jestico + Whiles

Over the past few years, the London-based firm Jestico + Whiles has enjoyed a fruitful and ongoing relationship with the UK Malmaison hotel group. The thread of the work has been to interpret Malmaison's core values in a variety of northern locations. The Birmingham hotel, their first in the Midlands, was unique in that, instead of adapting an existing hotel, it was located in a 'new' building. The canal-side Mailbox building, however, is new only in the sense that the old Royal Mail sorting office had already been converted into a large retail and leisure adaptation. The layout, however, offered the designers a new level of flexibility.

Malmaison's overarching style is 'inspired' by the 19th century French Château Malmaison, located just outside Paris, which is an elaborate piece of architecture that might at first seem a rather pretentious model for a mainstream UK hotel chain with premises in Edinburgh, Glasgow, Newcastle and Manchester. Jestico + Whiles have tactfully accepted this challenge and repositioned an essentially flamboyant concept of luxury in a more restrained and contemporary way. Another design aim of the Malmaison chain has been to infuse each hotel with something of the character of its location. In Birmingham, a city long over-shadowed by a post-war rebuilding programme of unparalleled hostility, this can be seen to have posed something of a challenge. Birmingham may claim to have more miles of canal than Venice but it is for good reason that Venice never claims to have almost as many miles of canal as Birmingham. This said, the Birmingham Malmaison is another step in the right direction of reinventing England's second city for the 21st century.

The Mailbox building's steel-framed shell allowed Jestico + Whiles unusual latitude, which led to the development of some large public spaces within the hotel. The building is entered from a newly created street (intended to unify the whole Mailbox complex) into the ground floor, which houses both the hotel reception and a holistic spa. The entrance lobby is clad in fumed and limed oak panels, incorporating Malmaison's signature detail of mirrors that contrast with the polished, dark-stained cabinetry. A grand spiral staircase (a reference to the staple feature of the grand châteaux evoked by the hotel name) features an illuminated wall of raspberry red glass and winds through the lobby leading to the next floor where the brasserie is located. On a mezzanine above the brasserie is the conference facility.

The 189 guest rooms on the six floors above are furnished in low-key contemporary style and feature photographs of Birmingham's industrial structures, which, in the main, tend to be rather less photogenic than those of Edinburgh or even Newcastle. However, for all its traditionally poor press, Birmingham was once the workshop of the world. A heavy industry giant at the heart of the Industrial Revolution, today it is an increasingly well-appointed city and, a vibrant meeting point for international business conventions and exhibitions. The city may have suffered badly at the hands of the developers in the 1960s and it may also have been dangerously slow to adapt to the terminal decline in its manufacturing base, but if it is now looking confident again, this is in no small measure due to its ever-improving built environment. In its own way, the Malmaison makes a small but worthy addition to that environment.

ABOVE

The lobby of Birmingham's Malmaison sets the tone for Jestico + Whiles' modern take on traditional luxury, delivered in a cool and restrained style.

RIGHT

Although not strictly a 'new' building, Birmingham's Malmaison was the first in the chain to enjoy relatively free spatial flexibility within the adapted mail sorting office building now known as The Mailbox.

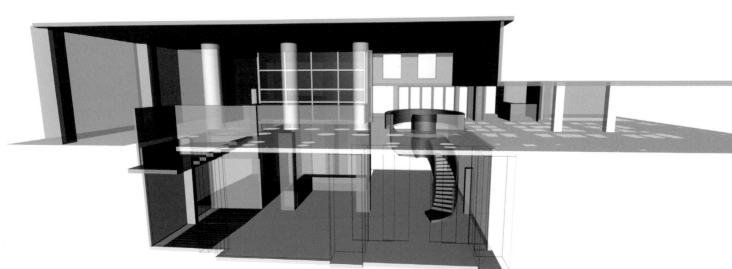

ABOVE

A stylish guest room, one of 189 furnished in low-key contemporary style and many featuring archive photographs of Birmingham's more famous industrial structures.

RIGHT
This plan shows the straightforward geometry of Malmaison's space within the Mailbox complex. The hotel shares the ground floor with a holistic spa.

FAR RIGHT
The staircase echoes Birmingham's past role as the workshop of the world. Its scale, shape and detailing evoke the lineaments of heavy industry without sacrificing the all-pervading sense of style.

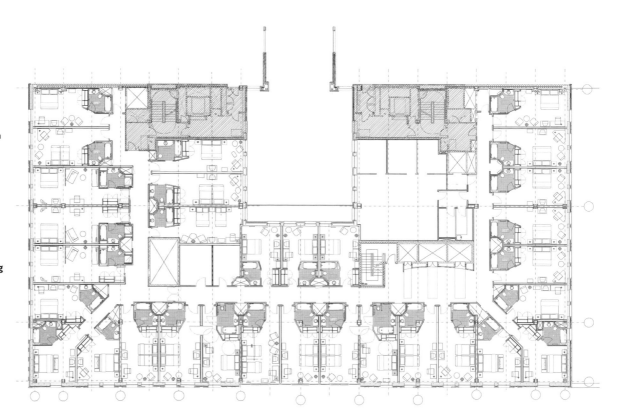

**A contemporary take on luxury. There is an architectural
dimension to this striking seating area in Malmaison's lobby.**

Le Meridien Minneapolis

Minneapolis, USA 2003

Architects: Antunovich Associates

Interior Design: Yabu Pushelberg

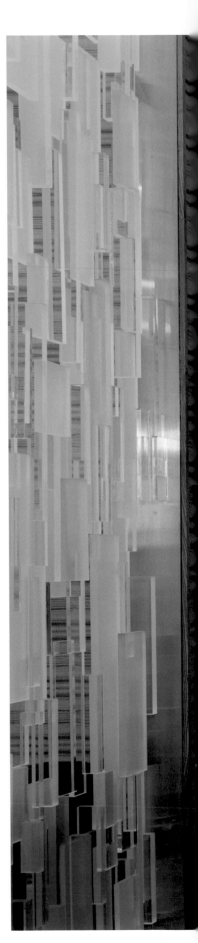

There is a strong mainstream theme to the story of Le Meridien Minneapolis, despite the decidedly cutting-edge reputation of its interior designers, Yabu Pushelberg. It is not that their dramatic reinvention of the hotel's public spaces is at all safe, rather that Minneapolis, despite its deserved reputation for artistic awareness and creativity, is not exactly the style capital of the world. The Meridien project grew out of what was a chronically difficult urban site. Block E was a real-estate problem child, one that most major cities have in some form or another. A series of aborted planning ambitions meant that, despite its respectable general location, Block E had become a sinkhole for petty crime and drug-dealing. At one point it almost became a parking lot but then Minneapolis's native commercial instincts took over.

The city that produced the legendary The Mall of America eventually decided to also turn Block E into another mall, above which rose Le Meridien Minneapolis's 22-storey hotel, its unremarkable, routine entrance flanked mundanely by a Hard Rock Café and a Starbucks coffee shop. Le Meridien Minneapolis is owned by Graves Hospitality who had already decided on the design of the guest rooms when they hired Yabu Pushelberg to give their 2,925 square metres (31,500 square feet) of public space what Glenn Pushelberg calls a sense of 'a hotel that projects confidence and professionalism as well as creative spark'.

If the hotel façade and its immediate surroundings are lacking in dynamism, the same cannot be said of the lobby where a sense of movement immediately dominates. Here, shimmering bronze slabs decorate some of the walls, grainy *paldao* wood veneers clad others, while the creamy Italian stone floor is veined with green stripes. Yabu Pushelberg decided to use a recurring spatial idea that involves leading the guests through a series of spaces that are located in most of the public areas, a device which Pushelberg suggests enhances the overall sense of space. '[Guests] have to pass through a series of spaces with corners and edges,' he says. 'If everything were opened up, it wouldn't seem as expansive, it wouldn't be as elegant.' The lobby space was divided into a seating area and a bellman's area. Guests wanting to use the elevators have to walk through both areas in order to reach it. A similar arrangement reappears in a ground floor nightclub (The Infiniti Room), a restaurant (Cosmos) and the hotel conference rooms. Screens, frames, dividers and slabs are everywhere, creating a richly textured series of connected spaces that bring a theatrical but legible quality to what might easily have become soulless utilitarian spaces in other hands.

The Yabu Pushelberg approach to what might have seemed an intransigent problem was to energize the public spaces by combining an architectural sensibility with interior design flair. Their delight in juxtaposing unexpected things – mirrored discs, corrugated glass, acrylic slabs, Italian marble, blackened steel, artworks that employ sandblasted woodblock or recycled paper – distinguish their work from that of lesser designers for whom the concept is sometimes more important than the quality and richness of the finish and materials. Le Meridien Minneapolis, with its 'Anytown, USA' exterior and its routine and somewhat predictable guest rooms, may not be a holistic design success but Yabu Pushelberg have certainly given its guests a dazzling series of public spaces to enliven their stroll from sidewalk to bedroom.

RIGHT

A palace of style in an urban jungle, Yabu Pushelberg's reinvention of the Minneapolis Le Meridien's public spaces combines an intelligent use of space with dazzling textural effects.

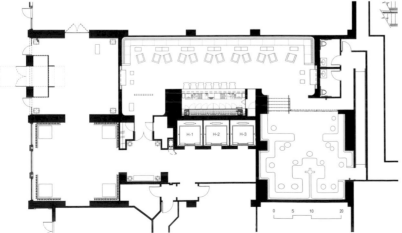

ABOVE
Screens, frames, dividers and slabs create a richly textured series of connected public spaces that lead visitors through what was previously a large and soulless area.

LEFT
Yabu Pushelberg's scheme of breaking up and articulating spaces is clearly visible in this plan.

RIGHT
Here, public space is used as an amphitheatre. No surface is undecorated, using materials that range from this warm illuminated panel to veneers, shimmering discs and even recycled paper fragments. Visitors can simply sit and look or work their way through this kaleidoscopic lobby to a nightclub, restaurant or conference room.

RIGHT
Le Meridien Minneapolis's dramatic bar with its radical Perspex seating.

ABOVE
The registration area with its illuminated backdrop art piece of tiny suspended paper fragments.

2 MAINSTREAM EXPERIMENTS

3 Original Ideas

Some hotels are born unique, some have uniqueness thrust upon them and others simply acquire it. A Canadian hotel constructed entirely of ice and snow, if not exactly unique (Sweden has one too), is certainly a structure whose appeal is indivisible from its novelty. A hotel for astronomers in a South American desert is a one-off for more accidental reasons: it is the logical coming together of purpose, location and climate that makes it so startlingly original. A German hotel for disabled people designed without any trace of drab institutional thinking ought not to be a rarity but, because it is the product of an uncommon alliance of social, political and design sensibilities, it is. Elsewhere, some hotels may simply embrace a quirky theme in order to reflect the appeal of some local attraction or evoke some aspect of their building's history. But whether they choose to borrow the visual manners of a Harvard library or give us a glimpse of life in outer space, the most successful usually achieve some inherent sense of design integrity quite independent of their theme or visual conceit.

The Library Hotel

New York, USA 2001

Architects: The Stephen B. Jacobs Group

Interior Design: Andi Pepper Interior Design

'Only in New York' is the all-purpose Manhattan response of amused resignation to any perceived local oddity, human or environmental. Could The Library Hotel, on 41st Street at Madison, only exist in New York? Probably not, but although semi-serious theming is a widespread American tradition, The Library Hotel combines marketing ingenuity with metropolitan pizazz and admirable attention to detail. Its designers have used the Dewey decimal system to 'classify' public and private areas; they have installed computer-controlled wall projections that announce a given floor's 'subject matter' as soon as you emerge from the elevator; and each of the hotel's guest rooms boasts bookshelves stocked with themed reading matter. Short of installing a doorman to whisper 'Sshh!' as you enter, it is hard to see how much further the concept could have been pushed.

Just in case the hotel name itself was not enough of a clue, interior designer Andi Pepper starts the theming early with a *faux* card catalogue at the front desk, following up with plenty of rich wood and some impressive floor-to-ceiling bookshelves. This is a hotel that takes its gimmick seriously and given the nature of the original building, the effects are not lightly achieved. Pepper's husband, architect Stephen B. Jacobs (whose firm specializes in adapting old structures for contemporary purposes), faced a fundamental problem of scale when converting the former office building. The 7.6 x 29 metre (25 x 95 foot) footprint gave a total area of 2,787 square metres (30,000 square feet) and made the design of the compact guest rooms a challenging exercise. Much of the furniture had to be built in, something that came naturally to Pepper and Jacobs whose personal enthusiasm for sailing meant that they were familiar with the space-saving tricks of a boat's living quarters. At the risk of overlaying a marine theme on top of a bookish one, they devised custom-built mahogany storage units incorporating various cabin-like features – tray-like tabletops that slide out and can be stowed away, for example. 'Virtually all of the furnishings had to be built in,' notes the architect, 'making this more like a yacht design than a conventional hotel.'

Mahogany-and-glass internal doors create a feeling of quality that offsets any potential negative responses to the smaller rooms. According to Pepper and Jacobs only two of the six rooms on a typical floor were 'smaller than we would have wished', but if the designers find a room too small then guests are even more likely to find the space limited. Then again, crowded New York is no stranger to small hotel rooms and The Library has certainly made the most of its available space with customized finishes and ingenious touches throughout. Any guest suffering from cabin fever can always go to one of the larger communal spaces. The main communal area is the Club Room on the second floor, which is a place that doubles as a kind of lounge and a breakfast room. Its tables and seating were designed to acknowledge the fact that guests consuming hot coffee and pastries do not necessarily want to be drawn into a semi-reclining position by squashy sofas and so the Club Room furniture works well in both of its roles. The roof also offers communal spaces; these take the form of garden terraces, a glazed winter garden and a hospitality suite. Design of the hotel's other public areas echo the exterior's Gothic-revival façade of tapestry-brick and terracotta to good effect.

At the time of writing this most distinctive hotel was marketing The Erotica Package, something that it had ingeniously managed to relate to its overarching library theme by inviting guests to visit the Erotic Literature Room: a conventionally designed guest room suitably dressed with props such as soft porn novels, erotic dice and champagne. This clever marketing idea further serves to demonstrate the resourcefulness of a hotel that is designed to make its individuality work for it. Only a few blocks away from the hotel, New York's most famous public library stands, still looking much as it always has done since it was built in 1911. So far, no one has attempted to theme it as a hotel, but then again libraries rarely face the same kind of competition as the hotel sector.

A small 7.6 x 29 metre (25 x 95 foot) footprint made this former office building at 41st Street and Madison a challenging exercise for conversion into a hotel. However, the Gothic revival façade of tapestry-brick and terracotta provided a distinguished starting point.

RIGHT

The Library Hotel's lobby establishes its theme with a *faux* card catalogue at the front desk, plenty of rich wood and some impressive floor-to-ceiling bookshelves.

LEFT

The narrowness of many spaces, such as this bathroom, was an inevitable result of the building's original configuration, although Jacobs and Pepper make a virtue out of a necessity with their calm, formal treatment and use of mahogany and glass.

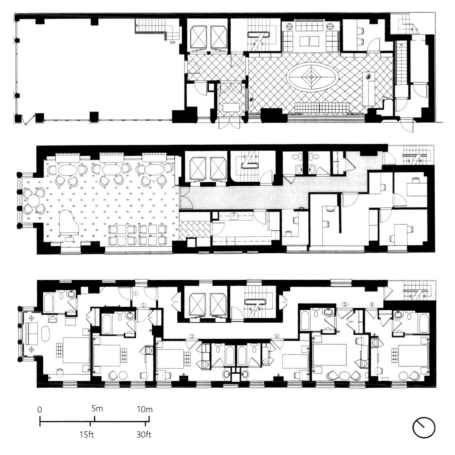

The library theme runs throughout the hotel although the individually fitted mahogany furniture with space-saving features, standard in all of the guest rooms, also recalls a well-apppointed but compact ship's stateroom.

LEFT
Three plans of The Library Hotel, showing, from the top, the ground floor, the first floor and a typical layout of one of the upper guest floors.

0   5m   10m

15ft   30ft

ABOVE

Not a feature found in many real libraries, the bar receives a curved and padded treatment that again recalls The Library Hotel's subsidiary marine theme.

LEFT

The Club Room on the second floor doubles as a lounge and a breakfast room with tables and seating equally suitable for casual dining and general relaxation.

Ice Hotel Quebec-Canada

Quebec, Canada 2004

Design: Ice Hotel Quebec-Canada Inc

The Ice Hotel Quebec-Canada is the only establishment in this book whose design is founded upon the fourth dimension. Time is very much part of this particular building since this hotel can only ever exist as an actual entity between January and April of each year – when the spring sun arrives and the hotel melts it is presumably prudent to make sure all the guests have been checked out. Between January and April however, even in this era of global warming, Quebec is confident enough of its consistently low temperatures not to fear an unseasonable warm spell that might result in the Ice Hotel Quebec-Canada turning into the Quebec Pool overnight. The hotel is therefore an annual event as well as a structure.

This is not the first commercial hotel to be built entirely of snow and ice – the original model was in Jukkasjärvi, Sweden, which has now been in seasonal business for over 10 years. The Canadian owners, Ice Hotel Quebec-Canada Inc, have, however, refined the concept and brought a certain element of North American marketing brio to the idea. Curiosity value is high here and there is an annual rash of special events that make the hotel a glamorous destination for corporate hospitality and private receptions as well as paying guests. There are 32 rooms and suites, a bar sponsored by Absolut Vodka, a chapel (the Ice Hotel may be seen as a kind of upscale, if sub-zero, version of Las Vegas for the purposes of novelty weddings), two exhibition areas, a large lobby illuminated by a fibre-optic candelabrum, a cinema and jacuzzis. However, by far the most interesting design aspect of the Ice Hotel is the process, both structural and commercial, by which it is repeatedly realized.

Architects, used to the protracted timetables of conventional design and construction projects, must weep to see the speed with which this 3,000 square metre (32,290 square foot) building, made out of 12,000 tonnes (236,200 hundredweight) of snow and 400 tonnes (7,874 hundredweight) of ice, is serially built. It takes 20 workers approximately one month to construct it, using stainless steel moulds and timber walls between which snow is blown and then allowed to freeze. Blocks of ice are used for interior structures, such as columns, the bar counter and furniture and also as bricks to line the ends of the hallways. Of course, compared with the contemporary design subtlety of the best conventional hotels, it can be said of the gimmicky Ice Hotel that its chief merit lies not in that it is done well but in that it Is done at all.

However, the strand of architectural thinking so long championed by the late Cedric Price (who firmly believed in the merit of temporary structures that responded to the changing needs of society) might draw support from the example of the Ice Hotel.

There are no big design names here, just an enterprising alliance between the owners, the Government of Quebec, the tourism bureau and their specialized teams of workmen. If the hotel's remit is narrow – there is, after all, unlikely ever to be a sister establishment in the Bahamas – its possibilities are theoretically very flexible. Each year there is at least the option to modify the Ice Hotel's capacity, to integrate new technology as it becomes available and to reinvent the same concept over and over again with improvements major and minor each time. What is more, the hotel's budget is founded upon the assumption of renewal, not burdened by provision for maintenance. For these reasons, The Ice Hotel Quebec-Canada is more than the curio it may at first seem. Furthermore, its use of recyclable building materials would seem to be unsurpassable.

BELOW

Construction of the shell of the Ice Hotel uses stainless steel moulds and timber walls. Snow is blown between the mould and the wooden wall and then allowed to freeze, after which the temporary elements are removed.

RIGHT

The Ice Hotel's Grand Hall achieves a surprising sense of cathedral-like space. Here, columns of ice provide internal support for the building shell.

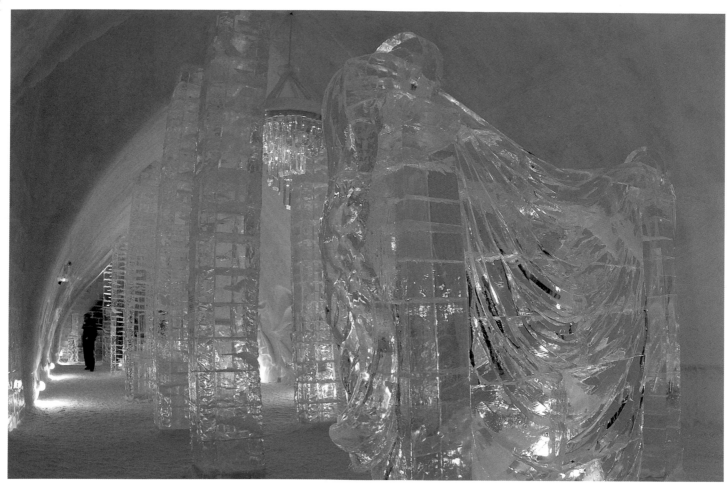

ABOVE

Sculptures and a chandelier demonstrate how ice can be used for sometimes quite surprising decorative effects.

RIGHT

A long ice corridor leading to the hotel's Grand Hall.

RIGHT

A booth carved into an ice wall, complete with a decorative bas-relief lighthouse that emits real light from its lantern. The seating units are insulated with reindeer skins.

RIGHT
**The Designer Room plays
host to a changing array
of sculptures and features,
such as this raised platform
evocatively lit from below.**

The Gran Hotel Domine Bilbao

Bilbao, Spain 2003

Architect: Iñaki Aurrekoetxea

Interior Design: Estudio Mariscal/Fernando Salas

The Gran Hotel Domine Bilbao is not the only hotel spurred into life by the city's acquisition of Gehry's spectacular Guggenheim Museum. However, it is the only one to bear the imprimatur of Spain's most famous pluralist designer Javier Mariscal. This is not to say that the Gran Hotel Domine is a 'designer' hotel in the usual sense of that phrase, rather that it has been uniquely branded as a celebration of design by its hotel chain owners, Silken Hotels, in whose crown it is the only five-star jewel. Obscurely described as 'a colourist microcosmos' in the promotional blurb, the 145-room hotel earns its one-off status not only by the unusual way by which its design credentials have been established but also by its museum-like collection of twentieth century household objects and furniture.

First and foremost is the almost tangible influence of the Guggenheim, which stands directly opposite. One of the Gran Hotel's façades is faced with mirrors to reflect dramatically the museum's extraordinary profile – no visitor or passer-by is going to be able to ignore the close physical relationship between these two buildings. The hotel's other façade responds to nearby buildings more conventionally but without entering into the excesses of some of its more florid, neoclassical neighbours. With the external scene set, the inside of the hotel reveals a cooperative vision, driven by but not executed by Estudio Mariscal. As the Spanish newspaper *El País* once noted, 'Mariscal is thought of as a kind of blender, in which Calder and Vázquez, Miró and Mickey Mouse, Matisse and Crumb are found in equal measures.' Silken Hotels probably thought that this kind of exuberant eclecticism is best mediated when it comes to hotel design, and so interior designer Fernando Salas implemented most of the designs after long consultation with Mariscal. Architect Iñaki Aurrecoetxea oversaw the construction process.

The design collection idea stems from the idea that, seen from the vantage point of the start of the twenty-first century, it was possible to take an overview of the international design trends of the preceding century and represent them with examples that are meant to be used and not just admired as in a museum. In broader visual terms the Gran Domine reflects Mariscal's input mainly in the integrated detailing. From staff uniforms and carpet colours to silverware, stationery and bedding, everything has been imaginatively co-ordinated. Even the hotel website was conceived as part of the overall design vision. The design of the hotel spaces reflects a strategy that is intended to draw outsiders into the hotel as well as to satisfy its guests. Cafeteria, cocktail lounge, restaurant, reading corner, hall, lounges, atrium and terrace have all been conceived as discrete spaces. Although they are linked, each has its own ambiance so as to encourage destination visits. The intention is to make the hotel itself a social hub for the city, while offering its guests the sense of excitement that comes from staying at a dynamic, fashionable address.

The rooms – 131 bedrooms and 14 suites – occupy five floors. Each room features a design detail that makes it individual and each floor is colour-coded with a different colour, which extends into the rooms and suites themselves. Mariscal designed the dedicated Domine lamp for use in the rooms and also the headboards of the beds. The hotel's design credentials are reinforced with a bath by Philippe Starck, faucets and other plumbing appliances designed by Arne Jacobsen and a stool by Alvar Aalto.

The cafeteria – Le Café Metropol – nods in the direction of the Bauhaus with pieces by Gropius, van der Rohe, Le Corbusier and Breuer, while the main hall, an arcade-like entrance space, features a giant red sofa created by the building's prime design motivator, Javier Mariscal. Overall, the Gran Hotel Domine is a carefully calculated team effort between owners, architect, a prestigious design guru and skilful interior designers. Complementing the Guggenheim with a design museum-based conceit of its own, it demonstrates how even an established chain can create a one-off hotel that responds to its specific location and the expectations that arise from having a uniquely prestigious neighbour.

RIGHT

Mariscal's 'take-no-prisoners' approach to hotel décor ensures that visitors are in no doubt that The Gran Hotel Domine Bilbao is not a natural choice for a quiet and restful weekend break.

BELOW LEFT

Bilbao's newest attraction, the Guggenheim, stands directly opposite. It is intermittently visible from various parts of the hotel and also stands dramatically reflected in the hotel's mirrored façade.

ABOVE
To sit in the bar of the Gran Hotel Domine is to blend into a stylish design tableau. This is just one of several discretely designed spaces, each a potential destination in its own right.

ABOVE:
The base of a massive stone sculpture within the lobby that rises into the atrium.

LEFT
One of the guest bathrooms. The bathtub is designed by Philippe Starck who has managed to give a distinctive new profile to a mundane piece of bathroom furniture.

RIGHT
Rooms facing inwards, into the hotel's atrium space, do not overlook the Guggenheim, although they do get a good view of Javier Mariscal's soaring stone sculpture that penetrates the building's lobby at ground level.

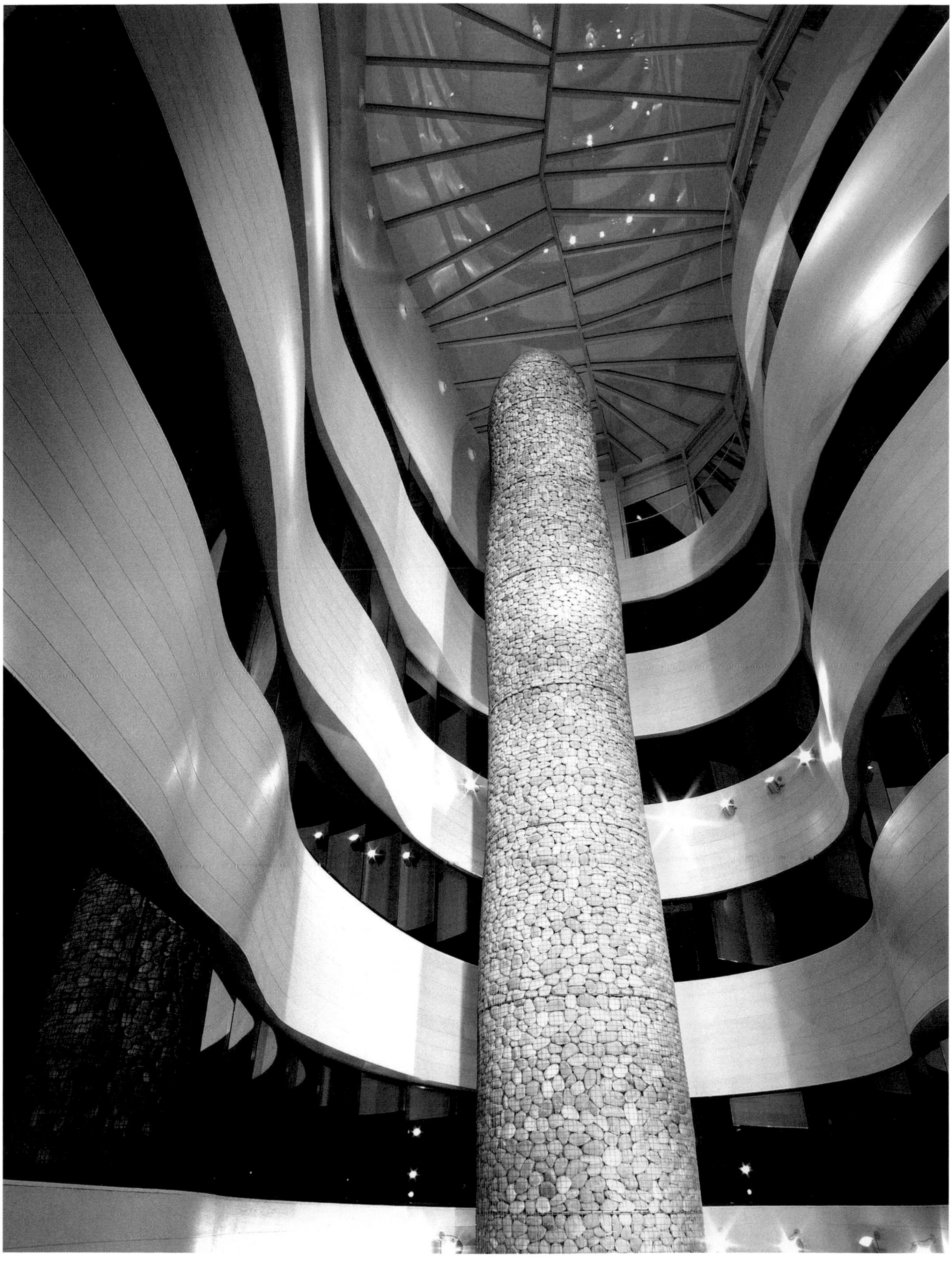

ESO Hotel

Cerro Paranal, Chile 2002

Architects: Auer + Weber + Architekten

Located in northern Chile's Atacama Desert at the coastal location of Cerro Paranal, some 130 km (81 miles) south of Antofagusta, can be found a hotel like no other on earth. The European Southern Observatory (ESO) has an outpost here sited at an elevation of 2,600 metres (8,530 feet) above sea level, on top of a small mountain. The numerous astronomers who visit the facility may be preoccupied with the unearthly things they view through the facility's telescope but, just like anyone else, they have mundane needs and a place to stay is one of them.

In a desert hollow at the foot of the mountain lies the ESO Hotel, designed by the Munich-based firm of Auer + Weber + Architekten and engineered by Mayr + Ludescher, also based in Munich. It is a 'trade only' hotel, catering only for professional astronomers and not the general public, a restrictive policy that might attract the attention of civil liberties groups were its motivation not so obviously innocent. For no one goes to this particular remote spot unless it is to attend the ESO facility. Although a tourist hotel exists not too far away at San Pedro de Atacama, it is Auer + Weber + Arkitekten's L-shaped ESO hotel that is the locale's real object of desire, seemingly occupying an almost elemental space in the desiccated landscape. Designed with elegant austerity, it is subtly integrated into the topography with its entrance buried at the end of a shallow ramp leading down from the desert itself, its red oxide-pigmented concrete walls keeping a low, warm profile in the desert. The design brief had reflected the fact that a conventional high-rise building would look absurdly dislocated in such a featureless landscape. It also reminded the designers

that harsh sun, lack of vegetation, powerful winds, cold nights and the odd earthquake would place even more demands upon the proposed hotel.

The result is a land-hugging structure in which necessity seems to have been transmuted into effortless style. The 108 bedrooms are arranged in serried rows that reflect the institutional connections of this particular hotel without ever descending into the dispiriting production values concomitant with so many publicly funded institutions. A circular courtyard features cacti, palm trees and an oasis-like swimming pool – this area is contained by a geodesic dome of translucent polycarbonate panels to provide essential shade from the searing desert sun. If this courtyard is the oasis within the ESO Hotel, then the hotel itself can be seen as an oasis in the harsh desert landscape.

Once, mirages caused by the heat haze would trick exhausted desert travellers into mistaking dislocated patches of sky for fresh oases that would disappear as they drew near. The ESO Hotel may in time also disappear but for more pragmatic reasons. Large government-funded Pan European ventures like this are famous for running out of money, impetus or even relevance, and yet if the ESO Hotel ever does become decommissioned it does stand a better than average chance of being adapted into a tourist hotel or some other less specialized facility. Its modular construction and land-hugging profile mean that it would easily lend itself to reconfiguration, while the use of local building techniques further enhance the possibilities of a possible adaptive use. It might then attract the wider range of visitors that its present use excludes but that its distinguished design perhaps deserves.

ABOVE

Set very low in the landscape, ESO Hotel minimizes its visual impact on a terrain devoid of tall buildings, trees or other prominent features.

RIGHT

Guests, all professional astronomers, can view the hotel surroundings almost as if from a fortified structure. Here, though, the fortification is against nature: strong sun, powerful winds, cold nights and the occasional earthquake.

LEFT

A room with a view – none
of the professionals staying
at the ESO Hotel expects a
short walk to the beach or
easy access to shops and
restaurants. There is,
however, a tourist hotel
not too far away at
San Pedro de Atacama.

ABOVE

A geodesic dome of translucent polycarbonate panels provides shade from the desert sun, while a circular courtyard within features cacti, palm trees and a swimming pool.

LEFT

A guest room of simple, elegant austerity – what more would you need with a view like this?

RIGHT

Ramps are used not only to give access to the hotel from the desert but also between the levels of this low-rise hotel. This contrast with the vertical expansion of most urban hotels adds another pleasing distinction to Auer + Weber + Architekten's building.

HausRheinsberg Hotel am See

Rheinsberg, Germany 2001

Architects: Dr. Pawlik + Partner Gbr

Interior Design: Mahmoudieh Design

This exceptional hotel, 60 kilometres (37 miles) outside Berlin and specifically designed for disabled people, tackles a genuinely difficult problem with some style. One of the fundamental aspects of designing environments for people with a disability is the need to design in an inclusive way. Inclusion involves not only practical elements that will extend and invite the usability of what is being offered, but also the handling of psychological elements, so as to avoid any hint of the inadvertent condescension that can so often mar well-intentioned schemes.

HausRheinsberg Hotel am See is a guesthouse that combines the comfort of a holiday resort while still addressing the special needs of its handicapped guests. Conceived by The Fürst Donnersmarck-Foundation in Berlin, the hotel was intended to reflect the new post-Berlin Wall social sensibilities of the German state. It eventually found its ideal location at Rheinsberg when a 14,000 square metre (150,700 square foot) lakeside

property came up for sale. The architectural practice was commissioned and subsequently designed a hotel complex with three guest wings and one central building, consisting of common spaces that include a restaurant, seminar rooms, swimming pool, fitness centre, bowling alley and a large multi-purpose hall. The ultimate aim was to realize a flexible barrier-free hotel for handicapped guests with 110 guest rooms and more than 150 beds.

The task of making the interior design match the aspirations of the scheme fell to Mahmoudieh Design, a practice with offices in Berlin, London and Barcelona. Yasmine Mahmoudieh committed herself to an aesthetic that 'does not show that it was planned for the disabled'. The recurring motif was a curvilinear form that was applied to cabinets and other fixed objects in order to avoid sharp edges and corners that could cause injury to someone with impaired vision or wheelchair users. Ceilings picked up the curvilinear theme, with wood panelling and indirect lighting, while natural circulation was encouraged by the curved elements that were intended to 'lead' guests through the internal spaces. The colour scheme Mahmoudieh used was intended to create a warm Mediterranean atmosphere to offset the grey surroundings on sunless days. The actual colours chosen were also good for the vision-impaired.

The surfaces were covered in a specially sourced scratch-resistant paint and wooden walls were given the additional protection of hardwood strips. In fact, wood features heavily despite Mahmoudieh's usual fondness for stainless steel fittings. 'I did not find stainless steel appropriate for this hotel,' she says, 'since it reminds me of surgical tools and hospitals in general'. The indirect lighting of the ceilings is carried through to the guest rooms with cut-outs incorporating a translucent material for lights in the walls and cabinets.

In everything from pool access (Mahmoudieh used a slide instead of the conventional high edge used in pools for the disabled) to subtle adjustments of furniture height and accessibility, the interior design incorporates its special features unobtrusively while seizing the opportunities afforded by the brief to use the chosen colours, shapes and materials in a celebratory way. A consistently (and unexpectedly) high level of bookings seems to have justified the entire HausRheinsberg Hotel am See project, from its visionary conception and funding through to its thoughtful architecture and interior design.

LEFT
The main entrance to Haus Rheinsberg am See. From the outset, the building evokes openness and light in an inclusive design treatment far removed from the stark institutional look too often associated with facilities for people with disabilities.

ABOVE

The layout of the restaurant successfully combines wide-access circulation corridors with the welcoming vernacular of a conventional dining area. Banquettes and casual groupings of chairs create a relaxed and informal feel.

LEFT

Space, light and the circular form of the hotel's foyer anticipate the design theme of HausRheinsberg Hotel am See. Curved walls and corridors throughout help to define circulation routes and minimize accidental impact with hard edges.

3 ORIGINAL IDEAS

A conference area is sited at the end of a broad corridor that has been designed for easy access. Seating around a semi-circular table faces two VDU screens.

Access to the hotel pool incorporates a spacious circulation corridor that is separated from the pool edge by some supporting columns.

Vigilius Mountain Resort

Meran, Italy 2003

Design: Matteo Thun

RIGHT

The sun terrace, a stepped, wood-slatted area that typifies the architect's bid to make timber the unifying material between the built environment and its natural surroundings.

BELOW RIGHT

Extensive timber louvres on the windows 'allow variable sun protection and natural regulation of the temperature'.

The Vigilius Mountain Resort represents a kind of Tyrolean equivalent of the Mii amo Spa in Arizona (see pages 222–227). The hotel can only be reached by funicular access, some may consider this to be inaccessible but others see it as way of ensuring its remoteness, as a result, like Mii amo, it is situated in a stunning natural setting with distinctive architecture that complements its surroundings. The line in marketing-speak, however, does, on occasion, defy belief and sometimes even comprehension – according to the brochure, 'the large windows allow a positive energetic balance permitting the exploitation of solar energy', which presumably means the windows have glass in them, allowing sunlight to pass through. There is plenty more of this sort of thing, all in support of a dubious eco-friendly philosophy that is so solemnly deferential towards nature that you might wonder why the client, Ulrich Ladurner, wanted to build a reinforced concrete and prefabricated wood hotel here in the first place.

He did, however, and hired Matteo Thun to supply a structure that, even the architect himself claims, 'from the outside, you hardly notice'. Carried away with the invisibility of his own work Thun goes on to say, 'when you're inside, you see so much you could be outside'. In fact, stripped of the rhetoric, the Vigilius Mountain Resort is exactly that – a resort in the mountains, 1,500 metres (4,920 feet) above Merano and conceived as an extension to a brand new hotel that was built to replace an old hotel on the same site, the Vigiljoch, as well as being a provider of new infrastructure for itself and the surrounding area.

In extending the existing hotel, Thun put the new three-storey structure on a North/South axis and embedded it low in the landscape. With its roof garden further helping to disguise it (and insulate it), the 112,500 square metre (1,211,000 square foot) hotel reflects the traditional timber construction methods of the region and incorporates a new building, which replaces the old structure that was pulled down while retaining that original's volume and position. This new building is Restaurant Ida, built of wood recovered from a 300-year-old Austrian granary and so winning another brownie point for eco-friendliness.

The restaurant is just one of a suite of facilities that also includes a lounge, a conference pavilion and a swimming pool. All open up onto the natural surroundings through large terraces with loggias. Beyond them a system of pathways 'in a natural way' engages the building with its surrounding landscape,

allowing adventurous walkers to explore the wilderness beyond the hotel. The Paradise Garden is another bid to blur the distinction between the natural and man-made environment; this small green hill planted with larches is located inside the complex between the guest rooms and the spa. The spa, pool and sun terrace are spread over the three levels at the southern end of the building with the pool being half indoors and half outdoors. Most of the public spaces are on the ground floor while the basement level houses a solarium and hay baths (wet hay and thermal blankets envelop the reclining user in what is claimed to be an 'energizing experience'). The remaining floor has a multifunction room used for gymnastics or group treatments.

The guest rooms alternate with public spaces along the North/South spine of the complex. All rooms have internally heated stone elements that also act as dividers between the sleeping areas and the bathrooms. Meanwhile, horizontal adjustable timber louvres at the windows act like regular Venetian blinds. Except that here, where 'natural' is the buzz word, the louvres 'allow variable sun protection and natural regulation of the temperature'.

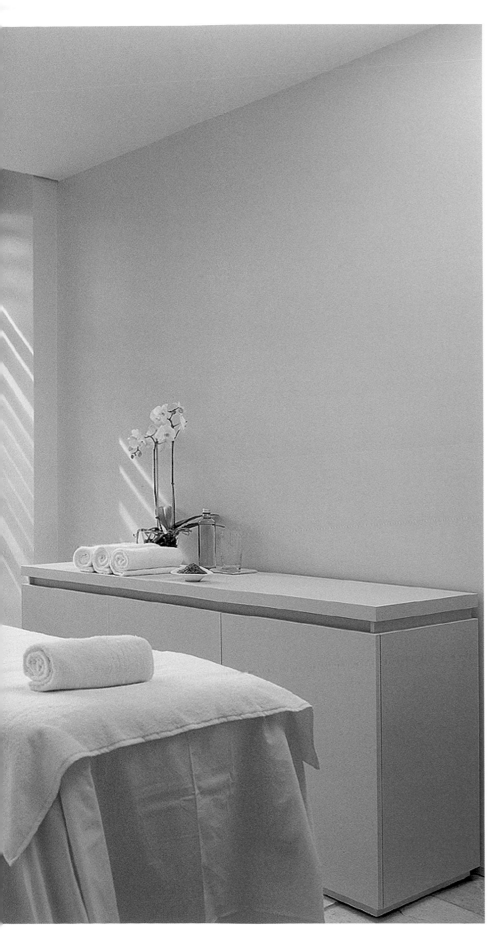

LEFT
From inside this a spa treatment room on a sunny morning, the value of the adjustable timber louvres can be appreciated.

ABOVE
Of the Vigilius Mountain
Resort the architect
suggests that 'when you're
inside, you see so much
you could be outside'.

RIGHT
Guest accommodation
favours restrained
elegance in the décor and
again makes generous
use of wood.

FAR RIGHT
Large stone slabs in the
guest rooms serve a clever
dual purpose. They separate
the bathroom from the
sleeping area and, being
internally heated, also serve
to warm the room discreetly
when required.

Alila Jakarta

Jakarta, Indonesia 2003

Architects: Denton Corker Marshall, Jakarta

The Alila Jakarta, owned by the Design Hotels group, has a simple and clear agenda: it seeks to embody the idea of the hotel as refuge, as a place of withdrawal, of calm and serenity. It is an image that for many years was, to some extent, enjoyed by Jakarta itself, but in one of history's little ironies the construction of the 27-storey Alila Jakarta (the name means 'surprise' in Sanskrit) was rudely interrupted by the political riots that erupted at the end of the 1990s. One design legacy of this unrest was that a new emphasis was placed on inward-facing glazing, looking out onto a central courtyard with its Zen-like garden of pebbles and tropical shrubs and trees. This offered valuable visual relief after a hasty battlefield design decision was taken to reduce the street front glazing because of the riots. In any case, the hotel's Central Business District location is a lively one by day and night, so the transition from urban bustle to a welcoming sense of calm as guests enter the double-height lobby is dramatized by the sudden contrast of surroundings.

Throughout the hotel, there is a complete absence of busy design features with most of the hotel's public areas taking a serene, minimalist approach towards both furniture and decoration. Denton Corker Marshall (DCM) also designed the lobby lounge furniture, which sits beneath a large Pieter Dietmar artwork using coloured timber strips in a rigorous rectilinear composition. Ceiling-mounted stainless steel pendant fixtures cast slivers of light onto floors of black Indonesian granite, while during the day natural light comes from the full-height windows overlooking the central courtyard. This courtyard is also overlooked from the opposite side by the hotel restaurant, the 150-capacity buzz Café, where DCM specified more spare furnishings including chairs of solid Indonesian *nyatoh* timber and black tables made of steel and anodized copper.

The signature colours of the guest rooms are saffron and crimson, their spicy and earthy tones mediated by restrained geometric shapes and DCM's unwillingness to introduce the slightest trace of fussy design or playful detail. These colours are featured in the drapes and on the massive fabric-covered, wooden headboards that extend upwards to the 2.5 metre (8 foot) -high ceilings. Once again, *nyatoh* timber is used for the furniture while another, darker indigenous wood, *merbau*, is used for the floorboards.

To the visitor from abroad the Alila Jakarta takes its place in the roster of international city centre hotels, and it acquits itself well in the role. In addition, it takes

as its entire theme that notion of personal well-being, which so many hotels separate and corral in their spas and gyms (the Alila Jakarta has its own spa and gym but its sense of well-being permeates all of its spaces). For the locals however, the Alila Jakarta also represents a first step in a new direction for Jakarta, a place caught between the old and the new and now taking its first steps towards reinventing itself in the context of a fast-changing world. It is one of South-East Asia's major urban centres, more liberal than some of its neighbours and with an atmosphere of noisy urgency to rival that of Hong Kong. In this context Alila Jakarta is interesting not just for the undoubted elegance of DCM's design but also because, unlike so many hotels that simply follow the urban pattern, here is one that is actually in the forefront of shaping the image of the city in which it operates.

RIGHT

Furniture that has been designed by the architects sits beneath a large artwork of coloured timber strips created in situ by artist Pieter Dietmar.

BELOW

By day, natural light comes from the full-height windows overlooking the central courtyard while at night, perforated stainless steel pendant fixtures cast slivers of light onto a floor of black Indonesian granite.

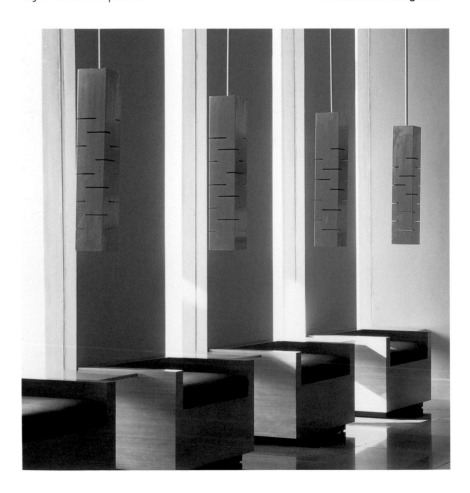

ABOVE
Saffron and crimson dominate in the guest rooms. The massive fabric-covered, wooden headboards almost reach the 2.5 metre (8 foot)-high ceilings. The floorboards are made of a dark indigenous wood, *merbau*.

ADOVE

After the front of the hotel lost its views due to security concerns, the focus shifted to this central courtyard with its Zen-like garden of pebbles and tropical shrubs and trees.

BELOW

Alila Jakarta's floor plan.

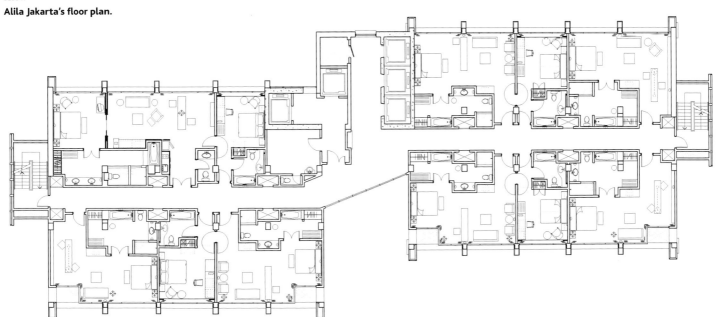

4 Designer Hotels

Gone are the days when 'designer' was a parvenu adjective used to describe anything that had aspirations to visual sophistication. Certainly you would be hard pressed to find anything at the cutting edge of today's hotel design that does not qualify for that accolade, outmoded as it is. Today, however, the phrase 'designer hotel' signifies something subtler and more varied.
It might simply signify the bestowing of a stylish imprimatur, as is the case with Bilbao's Miróhotel, which is credited to a fashion designer, or it may indicate that it fell to a designer to reinvent the concept of a hotel and turn it into an art piece, as with Matali Crasset's HI Hotel. Many other possibilities exist in between, reflecting the current elevated influence of the designer: the designer as Fashionable Society Figure; the designer as Artist; and the designer as Cultural Historian. The possibilities are many, although the day of the designer as Pioneer in a world of drab hotels is now gone. One might even argue that Starck, Putman *et al* did their 1980s trailblazing too well and that now their work here is, if not exactly done, at least done differently.

Miróhotel

Bilbao, Spain 2002

Architect: Carmen Abad

Interior Design: Antonio Miró with Pilar Líbano

The lure of a designer name combines with the nearby attraction of Frank O. Gehry's spectacular Guggenheim Museum to make Bilbao's Miróhotel a very desirable place to stay in the Basque Country capital. It is Antonio Miró's reputation as a fashion designer that has qualified him to come up with a hotel concept that is unashamedly art-driven and style-conscious. Occasionally overshadowed by the dazzling new Guggenheim, Bilbao's century-old Fine Arts Museum is also nearby and further adds to the expectation that most of Miróhotel's primary target clientele is the international art set.

The Miróhotel is a self-styled boutique-hotel with 50 guest rooms and a full range of amenities and services that include a spa, a gym, a cocktail bar and conference rooms. LCD TVs and DVD players are *de rigueur* in the guest rooms, since it is assumed that most Miróhotel guests will have these things in their own homes. Miró's main contribution to the hotel has been to specify a black and beige colour scheme throughout, using marble and leather from the local region. He has also inserted enough idiosyncratic touches to reinforce the idea that, for this particular outpost of Design Hotels International, there is no hint of a rolled-out design solution, just simply the stylish *imprimatur* of a national designer.

Velvet drapes hang at the windows and, in what the hotel promotional literature calls 'unexpected places', each guest room features a leather love seat and a distinctive square sink, designed exclusively for the hotel. Couples, comfortable with uninhibited domestic arrangements, can enjoy bathrooms that are integrated into the bedroom by simply drawing aside the curtain that separates the two spaces. Examples of art and design inhabit the public spaces with the hotel's own photographic collection taking pride of place. Here, the appropriate concept of a living art gallery is realized by providing a platform for local photographers as well as established international names, including Paul Thorel, Tessio Barba and Ana Laura Aláez. The overall interior mix is unashamedly one where, in the best European tradition, art, design and a chic lifestyle are treated as complementary and even interdependent. The marketing of the hotel fitness centre and spa, which offer 'ideal opportunities to de-stress body and mind after a day spent pounding the shopping streets of chic Bilbao', suggests that their perfect guest is unlikely to be a price-conscious office worker with a punishing schedule, waiting for a conference room to become free.

Miróhotel is both a branded hotel and a themed hotel, although perhaps not in the more widely accepted senses of those particular words. Fashion designers are rarely as well-equipped to design interiors as interior designers, but in this case it is merely enough that Antonio Miró has supplied catwalk glamour, a sense of international style and a subtle colour scheme. Hotels are not art galleries but it is almost inevitable that this one should showcase *objets d'art*. In the international consciousness art and culture have become an integral part of the appeal of Bilbao, and Miróhotel has staked its claim as one of the art-loving visitor's premium hotels of choice.

LEFT

The Miróhotel spa includes a massage area, Turkish bath and this elegant jacuzzi.

RIGHT

The hotel entrance on Alameda Mazarredo. From sand-blasted logo to stylized vegetation on sentry duty, the external signs and symbols are of coolly style-conscious self-awareness.

Guest rooms have a theatrical air, intended to challenge the traditional feeling of being in a hotel bedroom. This one offers a panoramic view of Bilbao.

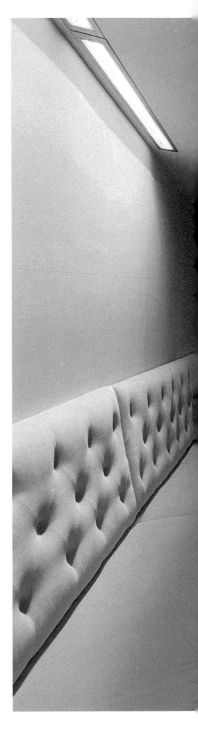

RIGHT
**The bar – a favourite
destination for locals
and guests.**

LEFT
**One of Miróhotel's more
conventional guest rooms,
where most of the bathroom
is hidden around a corner
instead of behind a curtain.**

Clift Hotel

San Francisco, USA 2003

Interior Design: Philippe Starck

Whenever Ian Schrager and Philippe Starck get together on a hotel project, things get interesting. Schrager's unerring instinct for the next trend is matched by Starck's particularly subversive brand of creativity, which views the reinvention of the wheel not as superfluous but obligatory. Any hotel (or restaurant or bar or lemon-squeezer for that matter) designed by Starck is unlikely to take the form-follows-function approach. Clift Hotel is therefore a predictably wilful inversion of the familiar luxury hotel concept.

The starting point was a 90-year-old building on San Francisco's Geary Street, a once glamorous hotel in the Italian Renaissance style that dated from a time when the city's European influence predominated. Well located in the city's theatre district and not far from Union Square, it was originally the concept of Frederick C. Clift, an attorney, who in 1913 commissioned the then 300-room hotel to be built on a plot of land that his family had inherited. Three floors were added in 1924 but thereafter, over the decades, Clift was successively renovated into mediocrity. The Four Seasons group were the hotel owners when Ian Schrager bought it in 1996. Starck's design approach was not simply to reverse this process and rediscover the original building's elegant bone structure, but to use the building as a dignified repository for all kinds of surreal and dislocated visual adventures, playing tricks with scale, historical period, colour and notions of art.

The soaring lobby houses an oversized floor lamp (designed by Starck himself) alongside another Starck-designed artefact – a sculpted Italian gilt and bronze chair of outsized proportions that recalls the kind of prop they used to use in movies before they were able to miniaturize actors with computer technology. A nearby Magritte-inspired stool, by Sebastian Matta, consists mainly of a bowler hat and a green apple and a working fireplace boasts a vast bronze bespoke mantel made by Gerard Garouste.

An original Clift institution, the Redwood Room, was once dominated by the colour of its redwood wall panels. In the renovated version this is virtually the only colour, repeated in everything: leather, fabric, carpet and metal; only the textures and finishes vary. Bursts of violet and gold and some flat screen video displays offer intermittent visual relief. Across the hall is the newly conceived Asia de Cuba restaurant. Adapted from an earlier cross-shaped room that was originally intended as an *hommage* to the Palace of Versailles, the restaurant takes its contemporary cue from the Redwood Room and features the same palette of colours with lush brown velvet curtains, custom mahogany, leather banquettes and dining chairs and a 10 metre (32.8 foot) etched and illuminated mirrored table.

Newly-arrived guests of a nervous disposition, perhaps secretly dreading bedrooms equipped with giant toilet bowls or steam irons armed with spiked soleplates, may be reassured by what turns out to be, by Starck's standards at least, a generally tranquil guest room treatment. Pale grey, ivory and lavender predominate although the sycamore sleigh beds are again of elephantine dimensions. Polished chrome sconces with pleated shades, a custom Venetian Murano glass standing lamp and filmy gauze curtains all add to the atmosphere of hazy drama. However, night tables of orange Plexiglas and floor-to-ceiling mirrors introduce touches of more overt theatricality but it never really compromises the generally calm and spacious ambiance of the rooms.

If one were looking for a signature detail to emblemize this particular hotel reinvention, it might be found in Clift's banquet rooms. Here the concept of classic banqueting seating has gone very post modern, with the use of moulded polyurethane, silver-legged chairs that sport slipcovers printed with etchings of Italian Renaissance chair frames. It might, of course, be argued that postmodernism is a bit passé in the twenty-first century. The joke inherent in ducking the chore of inventing a new aesthetic by playing tricks with old ones is perhaps wearing a bit thin by now but at Clift Hotel Starck does at least pull off the old trick with the consummate confidence of a past master.

RIGHT

Philippe Starck plays *Alice In Wonderland* games with Clift's lobby. His oversized Italian gilt-and-bronze chair sculpture forms the centrepiece for a display of eccentric and eclectic artefacts.

The Asia de Cuba restaurant is a new addition although it was adapted from an earlier cruciform room that was originally intended as an *hommage* to the Palace of Versailles, hence the cross-shaped tables.

Clift's guest rooms use a predominantly restful palette of pale grey, ivory and lavender. Their sycamore wood sleigh beds, polished chrome sconces with pleated shades and gauze curtains contrast with night tables of orange Plexiglas.

NEXT PAGE LEFT
A teasing glimpse from outside, through a doorway, reveals a Mondrian apple seat among an artfully arranged collection of cultural references.

NEXT PAGE RIGHT
The Redwood Room was a distinctive feature of the original Clift Hotel. The renovated version repeats the colour of the redwood wall panels in a variety of materials: leather, fabric, carpet and metal. Only the textures and finishes vary.

4 DESIGNER HOTELS

HI Hotel

Nice, France 2003

Architect: Frédéric Ducic

Interior Design: Matali Crasset

'[HI Hotel] may be the most important project for me', Matali Crasset said while she was still working on this rule-breaking Côte d'Azur hotel. 'It is global, a real hotel with music, images, art, a lively platform. For me, it is interesting because it is like making a never-ending object, which you use and then see how it can be changed from day to day.' Here is the essence of the unreconstructed designer thinking in relation to the designer hotel. In her mind, the place becomes an art object, a piece of self-expression, a personal project. Are art and design the same thing to such designers? 'I think that it is not interesting to understand whether it is art or design,' says Crasset unconcernedly. 'It is important to understand the approach.' It is an approach that can only thrive when someone rich and trusting is footing the bill.

In the case of HI Hotel it was Philippe Chapelet and Patrick Elouarghi whose restoration of Château de la Tremblaye in the Loire Valley won them critical plaudits but for whom the operation of a formal inland hotel soon became boring. In search of a new venture, better weather and sea views they ended up in Nice. There they found a 1930s building that had once been a boarding house and they hired Crasset, who had once been a pupil of Philippe Starck, to do radical things to it. The stage was set (the phrase is not an idle one) for a hotel awash with extravagant hyperbole and a series of hospitality experiences that owes as much to the fairground as to any conventional notion of board and lodging. The rooms, according to Chapelet and Elouarghi, are designed 'not as variations on an aesthetic theme but based on hypotheses for different forms of spatial organisation'. Not to be outdone, Crasset counters with the notion that the hotel is not ruled by 'an introverted, centrifugal force' but has instead been designed 'to stimulate curiosity, which can be bi-directional'.

Guests enter this avant-garde establishment by passing through a purple-tinted glass door and then between two low concrete walls, which have integrated speakers that issue constant rhythmic breathing sounds in stereo. A stylized revolving door (set to rotate '*adagio ma non troppo*') regulates the speed of anyone whose pace may have quickened in nervous response to the heavy breathing masonry, then there suddenly appears a richly colourful reception area and lobby with shop. A mezzanine loaded with books overlooks a double-height bar and dining area, at the far end of which is the sort of

basket that is usually found suspended beneath a hot air balloon or airship. Made of birch plywood it offers a kind of enclosure for guests who can sit on its leatherette-upholstered birch furniture.

'Throw out the hotel typology' had been Crasset's stated aim for HI Hotel and it was certainly one of her more lucid declarations. It was also the one to which she adhered most faithfully to throughout the project. Rooms would be not so much rooms as individualized concepts. 'Monospace' was the first, a three-stage living space each with a reassuring purpose: comfort, relaxation and natural breathing. 'Technocorner' became a room devoted to sound and images, a private AV haven featuring a sofa with built-in speakers. 'White & White' is a largely pigment-free room filled with furniture that metamorphoses into different furniture, thus a four-poster bed becomes a bathtub and a table turns into a bed, hopefully at the command of the guests. Most radically of all, 'Indoor Terrace' brings the outside indoors with a central patio-like living space separated from the room's shower by a plant screen and elsewhere featuring a toilet disguised as a garden shed. There are several more such playful inversions, all bouncing off the idea of a hotel as an emotional adventure playground rather than just somewhere to stay.

A rooftop swimming pool and a Hammam bath complex pose relatively few challenges to the norm although back at the 24-hour self-service restaurant, Crasset has once again been boldly going where regular designers fear to tread. Her white porcelain dinner service, 'Link', has a bowl for a cup, a teacup pressed into service as a soup bowl and so on. Just a few hundred metres from Nice's Promenade des Anglais, HI Hotel is an undeniable success judged by the brief it set itself. However, whether it finds a permanent place in the heart of this famous resort, once virtually annexed by an English aristocracy with traditional nineteenth century tastes, remains to be seen.

RIGHT

'White & White' is one of HI Hotel's several eccentrically themed rooms. Devoid of colour, it is filled with multitasking furniture: a four-poster bed becomes a bathtub, a table turns into a bed, and so on.

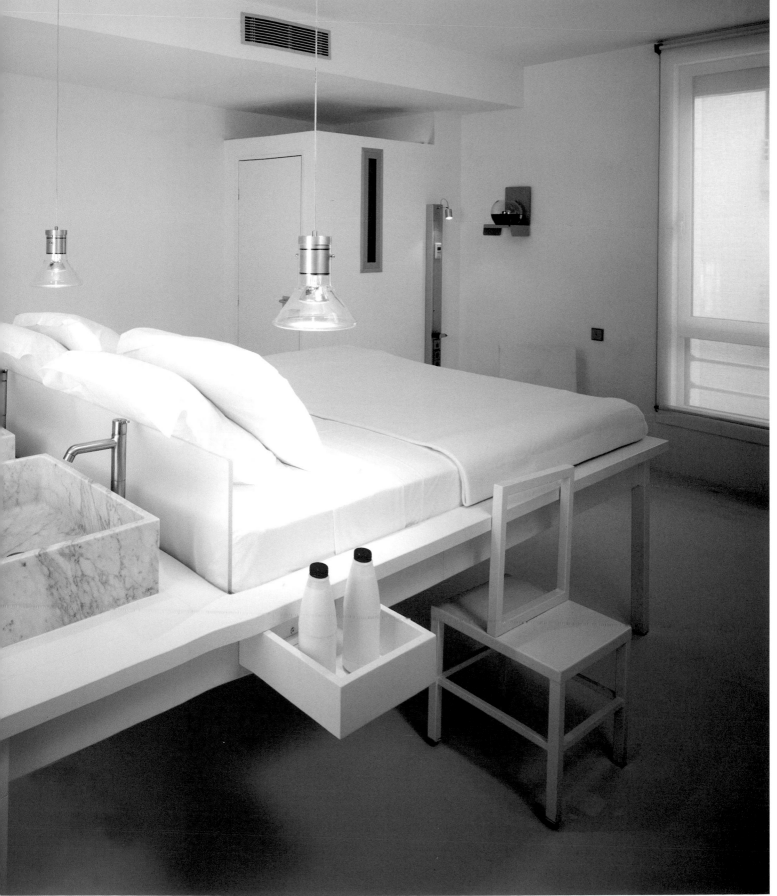

LEFT
The 'Indoor Terrace' room offers a central piano-like space as the focus of its bid to bring the outdoors inside. The shower is screened from the sleeping area by foliage and the toilet is installed in a garden shed-like enclosure.

RIGHT
'Monospace' was the first of Craset's room experiments. It is a three-stage living space dedicated to comfort, relaxation and natural breathing.

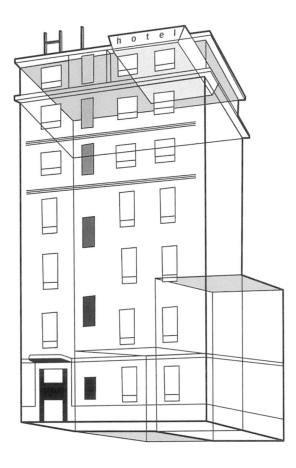

LEFT
A **3D plan** of the exterior of the **building**.

RIGHT
The **Hi Hotel's** Happy Bar with **its** slatted enclosure evoking the basket of a hot air balloon.

BELOW
'Digital' is a room with a cyber-culture influence. The walls evoke giant pixels and a **light box** is built into the furniture adding electronic images to the décor.

Continentale

Florence, Italy 2002

Interior Designer: Michele Bönan

The Continentale is one of a family of five hotels to be found in close proximity to one another in Florence. All five hotels are also to be found in close proximity to another family, the Ferragamos, whose decision to expand out of stylish footwear and into stylish hospitality via their hotel management company, Lungarno Alberghi SpA, was very much a design-led venture. From the top floor of the Ferragamo family's 13th-century headquarters (the Palazzo Spini Feroni) all five hotels are visible. They are located in a single city block bisected by the River Arno and include the Continentale, the Gallery Hotel Art, the Lungarno Suites, Hotel Lungarno and Palazzo Capponi.

The Continentale is the style cheerleader of the group, a grand renovation completely designed by architect Michele Bönan. The original structure was a 14th-century fortified tower that had been modernized in the 1950s; this latest makeover, however, has involved considerably more radical alterations. Exterior renovations include the installation of double glass doors at the hotel's two entrances and large new windows at street level and also on the first floor. Although the interior would be anything but historical in flavour, the courtyard façade was given a stylized glass and iron clock, a visual reference to a traditional Florentine type to be seen at many *palazzi* in the city and region as well as at the Palazzo Spini Feroni. Inside, however, it is a surprisingly different story, as the Continentale displays no postmodern reworking of fourteenth century effects.

To many designers, the 1950s remodelling might have been the first thing to get rid of. However, Bönan has actually chosen to celebrate a decade, which in Italy he says was 'A time of *haute couture* and real *luxe*'. Therefore, when guests enter from either side of the hotel, after passing through a cool and restrained welcome area lined with light grey Florentine stone, they enter a lobby tricked out with serpentine metal-frame chairs upholstered in startling hot pink. These chairs are reproductions although there are also some black-upholstered originals bought by Bönan from a local store.

The chairs are no fleeting nod back to the 1950s, there is more: a tall brass floor lamp, newly made but based on another period original; also to be seen in the lobby is the famous Egg, a suspended steel-framed wicker hanging-basket/chair designed in 1957 by Nanna Jørgen Ditzel. The overall effect – reinforced by a plasma screen showing old movies above a fireplace

and Faye Heller's monochrome photomontage featuring horizontal strips of heavily masacara'd eyes – recalls something of the visual vocabulary of Antonioni or Fellini in the 1950s and 1960s.

There are two reception areas, each with an individually designed desk (one is oak, the other zebrano wood and steel), a giant lift containing a sofa that prompts you to wonder how long it can possibly take to reach the modest height of the hotel's sixth floor, and a new oak staircase with a white balustrade. The public spaces extend upwards to the first floor where there is a breakfast room with tables and chairs by Arne Jacobsen sited behind the iron and glass clock. There is also a relaxation room with five Bönan-designed *chaises longues* from which to enjoy views of a city that, it seems, is increasingly being annexed by the Ferragamo family. Continuing up the building, the remaining five floors contain 43 guest rooms that are more restrained and even quite spare in their design. White walls and oak floors are enlivened with Bönan's version of an oak desk and chair whose steel and leather detailing suggests the reinforcements of an antique steamer trunk.

The Continentale ends with a flourish. What was once the bell tower is now a spacious suite, generously proportioned in every respect and with a private terrace affording sumptuous views of the Tuscan countryside. It is the unique topping on an architectural confection of some distinction.

RIGHT

Fifties pastiche chairs, Faye Heller's photomontage of heavily mascara'd eyes and Nanna Jørgen Ditzel's suspended Egg basket chair from 1957 combine to give The Continentale's lobby an eclectic retro look.

BELOW LEFT

The Continentale's courtyard façade features a dramatic iron and glass timepiece, a stylized visual reference to a traditional type of Florentine clock that is still to be seen throughout the city.

LEFT

A waiting area within the Continentale complements the lobby and comes equipped with its own evocation of the 1960s in the form of a fetishist cut-out sculpture.

ABOVE AND LEFT
White walls and oak floors characterize Michele Bönan's restrained treatment of The Continentale's reading room (above) and guest rooms (left).

BELOW

The breakfast room, with tables, chairs and five Bönan-designed chaises longues, from which to enjoy views of the city or to try to work out the time of day from the wrong side of the courtyard clock.

Pershing Hall

Paris, France 2000

Architects: Richard Martinet Architecture

Interior Design: Andrée Putman

'The idea of a hotel being a home-away-from-home is completely false, even absurd,' maintains designer Andrée Putman with characteristic certitude. 'Hotels should be like geishas. They distract and enchant you with their beauty, but they're not reality.' Perhaps this is the reason why, when it comes to hotels, Andrée Putman is the designer's designer.

Her landmark Morgan's Hotel in New York for Ian Schrager raised her international profile far beyond the design community but also reinforced her reputation within it. In 2000 she created the new face of Pershing Hall, formerly home to the American Legion in Paris, still bearing the name of its once owner US general John Joseph Pershing, turning it into a 'designer' hotel in every sense of the phrase. If, on its launch, the hotel failed to fill up at once with jet-setting US *glitterati*, it was only its post 9/11 sense of timing that seemed to be off. Everything else had been meticulously calculated and controlled by a designer in a position to make every detail bespoke and then to unify those details into an elegant and contemporary whole.

Pershing Hall, with its imposing Second Empire façade, takes a rather serene approach to the luxury designer boutique hotel concept. Next to the lobby is an eye-catching courtyard restaurant, theatrically landscaped by Putman who, with the help of botanist Patrick Blanc, turned an uninteresting, blank concrete wall into a soaring, vertical 34 metre 112 foot corridor of rainforest, rising to the top of the building from which a tropical cascade of vegetation seems to descend in a stream of sinuous vines, ferns, flowers and berries. 'It's quite amusing,' says Putman.

In the cavernous ground-floor lounge area and meeting space high ceilings serve as a reminder of the building's previous incarnation but by the time you get to the 26 guest rooms that encircle the garden, Putman is at her most minimalist. The rooms are intimate and not obviously in competition with any of Paris's grand palace hotel rooms, but Putman has made a virtue out of the constraint and concentrated on the detailing. Even the remote control for each room's DVD player is a finely detailed *objet*, not the familiar clunky lozenge. Decorated primarily in white with warm wood panelling, guest rooms feature some classic Putman touches, such as floor-to-ceiling mirrors, smart sliding doors disguised as mirrors and wood panelling dividers between rooms. The furnishings, all custom-designed, include square ceramic sinks, futuristic light columns, and beds with large cushioned headboards. Bathrooms with brightly lit bathtubs have plain, grey mosaic tiling and, in some guest rooms, feature oversized showers as well as free-standing tubs.

Beneath its tropical canopy the décor of the restaurant interior is fairly subdued with cream suede chairs and silver-mesh banquettes that seem to acknowledge the garden as the main atmosphere giver here and not the fixtures and fittings. A dual-level bar is even more austere. Discretion is the hallmark of Putman's interior treatment of Pershing Hall while preservation of the grand façade would seem to be the reason why street-facing rooms retain the kind of single glazing that pre-dated noisy motorized traffic. Rooms facing inwards to the courtyard are universally preferred by guests.

RIGHT

A balcony view of Pershing Hall's most dramatic feature: a soaring, vertical 34 metre (112 foot) corridor of man-made rainforest, rising to the top of the building's courtyard.

LEFT

An internal reminder of this Paris hotel's famous external feature.

PREVIOUS PAGE
The Pershing's split-level bar, showing the mezzanine section. The change of level introduces spatial variety in a building originally composed of large, high-ceilinged spaces.

ABOVE
The 26 guest rooms show Putman at her most minimalist. Decorated primarily in white with warm wood these are intimate rooms, far removed from the rooms in Paris's Grand Palace Hotel. The emphasis is on fine detail rather than grand gestures; even the remote control for the DVD player is a finely detailed *objet*.

LEFT
The front desk in the reception area of the hotel could be mistaken for two lecterns.

The dual-level Lounge Bar. Restrained and classy, the bar, like the restaurant, relies on its proximity to the spectacular vegetation in the courtyard for cachet. Note the ornate ceiling fixtures left over from the building's Legion past.

UNA Hotel

Florence, Italy 2003

Architect: Fabio Novembre

Fabio Novembre's conversion of an industrial building into a luxury hotel for the Italian hotel group UNA has given Florence's historic district of San Frediano a highly dramatic new space, dripping with the kind of interior design that could never be called understated. Fabio Novembre himself could likewise never be called understated and his commentaries on his own work seem intended to boost his reputation for eccentricity rather than to shed light on the design process. Accordingly, the Florence UNA is one of the latest expressions of Novembre's belief that the hotel is 'a spatial narrative touching on themes like the mobility of the planet, presence within absence and intellectual nomadism.' How this view sits alongside his other stated conviction that the UNA is 'a tree whose far-reaching branches extend across the world but with roots firmly embedded in its native soil' is anybody's guess, but such obliquity may incline us to mistrust his third declaration. 'Whatever [the UNA] may be' he claims, 'it is not a design hotel'. Of course the UNA clearly is a design hotel. It is a typically eclectic Novembre confection deploying diverse materials that include mosaics, leather and printed lamé. Guests know what they are in for upon encountering an entrance and reception area where a long loop-the-loop strip of mosaic tiling encircles, envelopes and guides them to the reception desk which is also absorbed into the mosaic treatment. Mosaic is a vernacular feature of Florence where it can be seen in many of the surrounding region's villas, although not quite like this. Novembre's loop motif continues into the bar area which is equipped with some similarly enclosing AND1 sofas from Cappellini. A restaurant has been conceived as a refectory, with a single long, sinuous table, designed by Dutch artist and architect Joep van Lieshout to bring guests together rather than keep them apart. The accompanying Shaker chairs and stools are by Atelier van Lieshout and aloft the restaurant's moulded ceiling echoes the line of the edge of the table with an illuminated 'stained glass' ribbon of light. The interior design does not stop trying for equally big effects even beyond the reception, bar, lounge and restaurant: it also invades the traditionally more restrained zones of corridors and guest rooms. Novembre is big on corridors, citing those in Kubrick's *The Shining* 'where the actors get lost running around the corridors'. His point, as ever, is unclear, but he seems to approve of disorientation since his treatment of UNA's corridors abandons room numbers altogether in favour of identifying the 84 guest room doors by sticking on reproductions of full-length portraits from the Uffizi Gallery. These tenebrous, life-sized portraits stand in funereal ranks beneath Dali-esque corridor ceilings that are all dark waveforms and ripples. Behind the doors the guest rooms feature mosaic again, with floors rising up seamlessly to merge into horizontal surfaces here and there, sleeping areas raised on platforms and a profusion of textures applied from everything to walls, counters and closets: black leather, rosewood and wengé panelling and fuchsia felt. Closet doors feature images of clothes on hangers.

In a rare moment of lucidity, Novembre will admit to theming the UNA on the Florence of Lucrezia Borgia and Machiavelli, a murky proto-*Sopranos* world of shadows, plotting, duplicity and death. As a hospitality concept it is original although it does have its downside. After a grappa or two in the bar, trying to walk along a mosaic tube where the wall suddenly runs round the ceiling may prove almost as disturbing as encountering a dimly lit corridor full of long-dead Florentines and forgetting whether your room key fits Anna Maria Luisa de'Medici or Giovanni Bentivoglio. As ever, Novembre has some helpful words for guests who might find his vision too intense. 'Life is a challenge,' he says. 'Living with a capital L is the hardest thing to do.'

RIGHT

A ribbon of spiral mosaic tiling encircles and leads the guest from the entrance to the reception.

LEFT

A sinuous, snaking table draws diners together rather than hiving them off onto individual tables. The lighting panel exactly echoes the lines of the table beneath.

LEFT
**The spiral theme,
begun at the entrance,
is dramatically continued
in this bar area that is
also equipped with
Cappellini sofas.**

A guest room showing the closet, complete with a clothes graphic, and the bed raised on its own platform. A variety of textures add richness to the room.

Two doors cleverly disguised as old paintings with gilded door frames instead of picture frames.

Soho House

New York, USA 2003

Architects: Harman Lee Jablin

Interior Design: Studioilse

Style writer turned practitioner, Ilse Crawford, left a high-profile career pontificating about design via *Elle Decoration* to become a designer in her own right with her company Studioilse. Seriously plugged into the international style set, she established a working relationship with Nick Jones, working on his Babington House (a British manor house transformed into a boutique hotel), The Electric Cinema (an old Notting Hill hippi haunt reinvented for the 21st century) and now Soho House, Manhattan.

This six-storey, 4,180 square metre (45,000 square foot) warehouse was transformed into a club with 24 hotel rooms, a restaurant and lounge, three bars, a screening room, a 'library' for private functions, a spa and a destination rooftop pool that was once even referred to by Samantha in an episode of *Sex and the City*. In contrast to the ephemeral kudos of being mentioned in a TV series, the robust 19th-century building was originally designed by Boring & Tilton, architects of Ellis Island's main immigration building. Harman Jablin Architects were charged with leaving visible many of the tell-tale internal traces of the building's history: brick with peeling paint, mismatched and reused floorboards, cast-iron columns, hand-cut wood beams and stripped wood ceilings.

The 'original fabric' consisted of brick walls, timber beams and the like. 'Without those great bones, it would have been impossible to create the mix of amazing modern furniture and amazing vintage pieces,' notes Crawford, whose capacity for amazement seems considerable. Soho House is at heart a club and its hotel element, although a separate offer open to the public, trades heavily on the club mentality. Its 24 rooms were designed to give guests a feeling of having their own 'dream apartment, without the responsibilities' according to Crawford who adds, apparently without irony, that an achingly hip Soho House guest room is somewhere you can go at day's end 'to relax without having to pose'.

There are four categories of guest room, all dedicated to the notion of play. For 'play' we can read 'sex', since despite all the coy rhetoric, Soho House is very much a calculated expression of the chic *Sex and the City* ethic, and it is revealing that when presenting her original Soho House proposal, Crawford played a typically priapic Serge Gainsbourg song, '*69, Année Erotique*'. Three 88 square-metre (950 square-foot) suites are designated Playgrounds, nine 70 square metre (750 square foot) rooms are Playhouses and nine more 39 square metre (420 square foot) rooms are Playrooms. Three Playpens, presumably for those who need even less room to play, are 30 square metres (325 square feet) each. The rooms owe more to the model of the Manhattan loft than the traditional hotel guest room. Studioilse has filled them with eclectic juxtapositions of elaborate and oversize marriage beds, leather-covered chesterfields, vintage *armoires*, modernist sofas by Piero Lissoni, Cab chairs by Mario Bellini and free-standing concrete bathtubs.

'In my experience as a magazine editor,' says Crawford, 'I learned that you need to combine the planned and the unplanned.' Accordingly, Crawford purposely waited to finish off the planned interiors of Soho House with chance flea-market purchases. On the rough painted-brick walls, she decided to leave test patches of colors ranging from peacock and teal to petrol blue-green. Her reputation is for combining and contrasting the objects she assembles in ways that represent an invigorating contrast to the internal effects of so many 'cookie-cutter' hotels.

RIGHT
The signature of Studioilse is a fashionable brand of eclecticism based on its principal's fondness for unlikely juxtapositions that tap into the Zeitgeist. Here, an exciting flower mural fights for attention with an Anglepoise lamp and a leather-covered chesterfield.

LEFT
An object of desire – 'There's a pool a block from my apartment – and I can't get in' Samantha (Kim Cattrall) once complained in *Sex and the City*. It was this one at Soho House. On this kind of cachet are hip designer reputations built.

RIGHT
A one-off guest room at Soho House illustrates just how far this kind of designer hotel is from the 'cookie-cutter' design solutions rolled out by the major chains.

RIGHT
One of Soho House's public spaces: a new take on the idea of the club.

LEFT
With the aid of another overblown desk lamp, Warren Platner's wire-frame seating and a velvet-covered sofa, Soho House manages to turn even its library into a dramatic space.

5 Architectural Significance

It is in the nature of hotels that the majority of revamps rely heavily upon interior design rather than architecture, which can be a slow process, inimical to the pressing agenda of hotel owner or developer. However, where good hotel building design is feasible, the results are almost always more satisfying than that which even the most inventive interior renovation can achieve on its own. From the subtle contextual solutions of Eva Jiricna and TEN Arquitectos to the dramatic polemics of Ruy Ohtake, architects respond in a variety of ways to the challenge of defining how a 21st-century hotel might look and operate. In one radical instance a distinguished but decrepit 1930s hotel has been faithfully restored and then provided with an entirely separate companion hotel building by way of modernization. In another, a mountain spa hotel, with a sales pitch based upon fulsome New Age marketing, profits from a rational design by a firm that is more used to dealing with the tight architectural constraints of urban public spaces. In all these cases the subsequent interior design at least had the opportunity of complementing and continuing the design message of the building itself and not simply creating an isolated milieu within an existing structure.

Hotel Josef

Prague, Czech Republic 2002

Architects and Interior Design: Eva Jiricna Architects Ltd

When Hotel Josef opened in 2002, it was more than just another Prague hotel reflecting the aspirations of a new republic. While the hotel's interior championed and advanced the idea of design-led hotels in the Czech capital, its exterior complemented an already architecturally rich neighbourhood in a city blessed with many distinguished buildings. London-based architect Eva Jiricna was born in Prague and the 110-room Hotel Josef, designed and built for her native city, would prove to be her biggest project to date.

Although contemporary Prague is a city with numerous examples of adapted buildings – some of considerable quality – this hotel was to be a completely new structure. As well as the obvious advantages this offered, such as permitting more control over internal spaces, it also raised the question of how to integrate a modern building into a tight urban context, largely defined by the ornate aesthetics of the 1800s. The site was situated near the Jewish quarter (Josefov) and a short distance from the city's Old Town Square, a small space formed by a T-junction of three streets and accompanied by a stock exchange, government buildings, bank headquarters and office buildings. Planning consent was granted for an eight-storey building that would continue the frontage of the adjacent buildings and whose roof would form a gentle transition between those of the buildings on either side.

Jiricna decided on a relatively featureless façade, a simple alternation of glazed areas and solid wall with the windows made as large as possible to make the relatively small guest rooms appear open and airy. To offset the risk of the façade looking too austere compared with its neighbours, Jiricna also specified lightweight perforated sunshades that, apart from protecting the guest room interiors from the summer glare, also added a three-dimensional element to the façade. By matching the height of an adjacent building to the right and then gently stepping down to continue the roofline of the lower building on the left, Hotel Josef's façade now plays an important role in holding the line of the street. As a result, viewed from the front, the hotel's appearance is light, transparent and contemporary. In fact there are two hotel buildings, the second is a linked building that is set back and offset from the first with a 102 square metre (1,098 square foot) recreational garden in between.

The ground floor and basement of the hotel contain the public spaces: reception, breakfast room and conference areas. With the particular geometry of its rectilinear window frames and other decorative touches, the breakfast room makes a quiet reference to the 1930s Czech Modernist style but the overall visual feel of the public spaces is a non-referential one of brightness and restraint. Staircases feature repeatedly in Jiricna's work and at Hotel Josef a spiral staircase with glass steps is used to introduce an atmosphere of lightness and airiness. It is worth remembering that Eva Jiricna has a dazzling international portfolio of design for shops, showrooms, nightclubs, stores and bars as well as architectural projects. This pedigree is reflected in the Josef's 110 rooms, where comfort and sophistication are the keywords even if compact proportions are the reality. In some rooms, in order to alleviate any sense of cramped space, glass bathrooms have been created using transparent screens or mirrored sliding doors in order to extend the illusion of space in the bedroom. Other guest rooms sacrifice this illusion for the increased privacy afforded by stone-clad bathrooms. Rooms on the top two floors also have terraces with views of the city to which Hotel Josef has now made its own contribution.

Jiricna, whose reputation might have led some to suppose that this grand project might be used as a 'designer' hotel *par excellence*, has in fact treated Hotel Josef with restraint both inside and out. Instead of shoehorning in an avant-garde architectural statement, she has given Prague an elegant demonstration of how to make a quality contemporary building coexist with its venerable neighbours, without being overawed.

RIGHT

Elegant staircases are one of Eva Jiricna's recurring signature features. At Hotel Josef her spiral stairs with glass steps introduce an atmosphere of lightness and airiness as well as providing a dazzling piece of utilitarian sculpture.

ABOVE
Light and airy, Hotel Josef's reception area sets the tone for a superb piece of hotel architecture that injects new life into the fabric of a city that is more used to adaptive renovations.

LEFT
Planning consent was granted for an eight-storey building that would link the frontage of the adjacent buildings and whose roof would form a gentle transition between those of the buildings on either side.

RIGHT
Space is at a premium at Hotel Josef and in some guest rooms bathrooms are designed with transparent screens or mirrored sliding doors in order to create the illusion of extra space.

The architect decided on a relatively featureless façade using a simple alternation of glazed areas and solid wall. To add visual interest and protect the guest room interiors from the summer glare, she also specified lightweight perforated sunshades for the windows.

BELOW
**Floor plans show the layout
of Hotel Josef.**

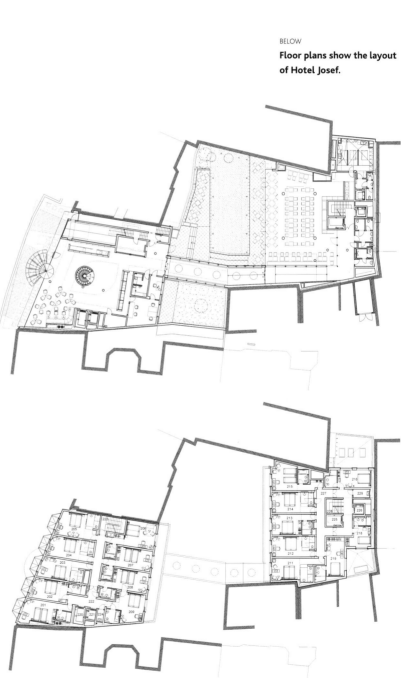

Radisson SAS Hotel

Glasgow, Scotland, UK 2002

Architects: Gordon Murray + Alan Dunlop Architects

Glasgow, long-term rival of Edinburgh in all things civic, has had a patchy reputation for urban regeneration, despite its tenure as European City of Architecture and Design in 1999. It was at that time that the Glaswegian firm of Gordon Murray + Alan Dunlop Architects (gm+ad) won a competition to design a five-star hotel on Glasgow's decidedly one-star Argyle Street. The site, near the city's Central Station, had once housed a tenement block and had been derelict for 15 years; it is said that only the brave were inclined to venture down Argyle Street after dark. The Radisson was therefore to be as much a hotel intended as a catalyst for urban regeneration as a much-needed city facility. The new building had to incorporate an existing structure (a B-listed 1905 Baroque-façaded building, designed by Steel and Balfour and situated on Robertson Street) into its new form and also pay its respects to other buildings in Argyle Street where the average height was around 20 metres (66 feet), a scale now redundantly determined by the reach of the Victorian fire ladder.

A single monumentally bold touch defines the Radisson SAS and is the key to its overall design approach. It is fronted by a huge 60 metre (197 foot) long contoured copper screen – a reference to Glasgow's historic use of metals and using a stylised prow shape evocative of the ships that were once made on the Clyde. The lightweight screen is supported on columns with glazing between them and rises to a height similar to neighbouring buildings, creating a street-level illusion that the eight-storey hotel standing behind it is lower than it really is. The columns, diamond in plan, and the glazing between them together create a corridor between the street line and the hotel interior. At its centre, a box-like suite of specialist rooms that cantilever out to overhang the pavement in a bold architectural gesture dramatically penetrates the copper screen.

The original plan had been for an eight-storey, 300-bedroom, five-star hotel - when Radisson was contracted as operator, however, the number of floors remained the same but a star was dropped and the room count went down to 250. Despite this, the quality of the broad hotel concept was undiluted and the theatricality of the exterior now gives way to an interior that introduces a sense of architectural formality, weight and dignity. 'As a counterpoint to the flexible and lightweight screen,' says Alan Dunlop, 'the main part of the hotel was designed to be solid, even monolithic, so we clad the walls in slate.' The solidity behind the façade is appropriate. Glasgow, a city that is reinventing itself as a centre for culture, cafés and conferences, was built on shipping and heavy industries that are now gone, if not forgotten. Substance and style seem, therefore, to sit well together.

From the inside, the copper screen affords intermittent views of some of Glasgow's other famous buildings, including a bank by Alexander 'Greek' Thomson. Inside, beyond the glazed entrance wall, the hotel foyer reveals a generous sense of scale, rising up to the building's full height with the lower areas of its main wall clad in dark timber rather than white plaster to give a more textured feel and to relate the towering space to a more human scale. This foyer houses the reception, a bar, a stairway to the first floor conference suites and meeting rooms, and a small bistro – all this is designed by gm+ad. Behind the foyer is a Spanish-themed restaurant, designed by Pentagram, which opens onto Robertson Street, and at the easterly end of the foyer there is a bar, situated on Argyle Street and designed by Graven Images. All of this suggests that the guest rooms might similarly have a first-class design input, however, here Radisson has implemented the strict design specifications that cover rooms and other elements of its chain.

The unique appeal of gm+ad's hotel was only made possible by an enlightened client, developer MWB (Marylebone Warwick Balfour Group plc), who set up the original design competition. That appeal, therefore, resides not in Radisson's 'cookie-cutter' guest rooms but in the hotel's public spaces and, perhaps most of all, in the external impact of this striking, land-locked hospitality vessel with its striking green prow.

The Radisson SAS Hotel's foyer reveals a generous scale, rising up to the building's full height. The lower areas of its main wall are clad in dark timber to give a more textured feel and a more human sense of proportion.

This end elevation shows how the new building had to accommodate a 1905 building by Steel and Balfour, situated on Robertson Street, while respecting the scale of other buildings on Argyle Street, where the average height was around 20 metres (66 feet).

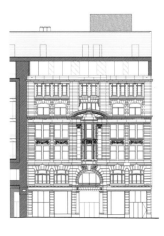

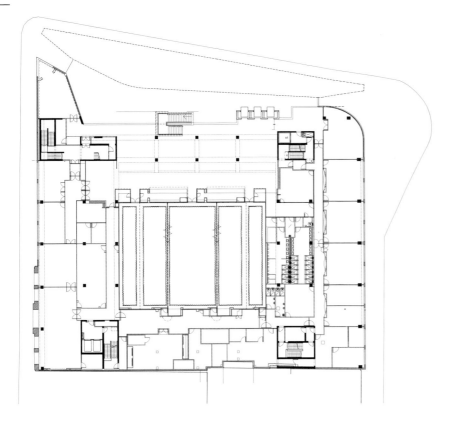

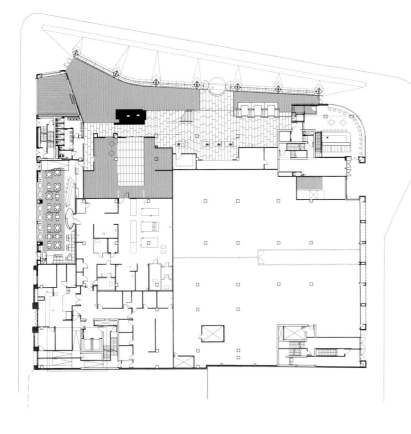

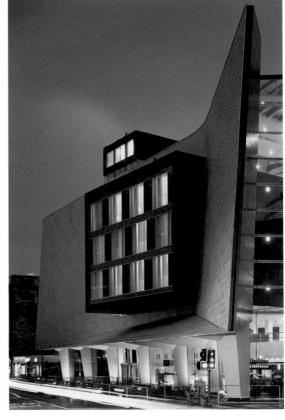

ABOVE

Full steam ahead for a Glasgow hotel that is happy to reference the city's shipbuilding past while creating an entirely contemporary building.

RIGHT

A stairway from the foyer to the Radisson SAS Hotel's first-floor conference suites and meeting rooms.

LEFT

Floor plans clearly show the layout of the hotel.

LEFT
A view into the atrium from a first floor corridor.

RIGHT
The atrium, seen here from the foyer, gives an open and airy feel to the hotel.

Hotel Unique

São Paulo, Brazil 2003

Architect: Ruy Ohtake

Interior Design: João Armentano

Hotel Unique, in São Paulo's Jardins district, is not a building that is easily over looked. Certainly if the city's 25-metre (82-foot) zoning height limit was meant to protect the neighbourhood from attention-seeking architectural intruders, it has failed spectacularly. For whether Hotel Unique reminds you of a 100-metre (328-foot) -long fruit segment, a giant antique ink blotter, a ship or an ark, what it does not particularly remind you of is a hotel. The plot was originally going to have a shopping mall built on it until the wealthy pharmaceutical heir Jonas Siaulys, who acquired the site, abruptly decided to build a boutique hotel instead. His chosen architect, 'Master' Ruy Ohtake, was so enthusiastic about the project that he delivered sketches within 48 hours, speedily seizing the opportunity to give the city a spectacular new landmark. Hitherto, São Paulo had lacked anything to rival the designer hotels of Los Angeles, New York and Miami, so Siaulys' decision was a golden opportunity for the Brazilian architect, who is second only in international fame to Oscar Niemeyer. 'I think he realized that the possibilities for a hotel were greater than for a mall,' says Siaulys. 'He knew that we'd give him creative freedom.'

Ohtake had already designed the São Paulo branch of the Renaissance hotel chain but Hotel Unique offered a chance to further his own radical agenda for the city's architecture and to push a hotel building as far as it would go, if not further. The idea was to combine monumental architecture with whimsical design and luxurious informality, although at least one member of the city's planning department at the time felt that the Hotel Unique was first and foremost an architectural *beau geste* from Ohtake. 'The Unique is a hotel by accident,' comments former municipal planning secretary Heloisa Proença. 'More than anything, it is Ruy's building.'

Ruy's building is based on a long inverted arch with two lateral concrete walls. Access to the hotel is through carbon fibre doors in the big wedge-shaped empty space to the right while access to an events centre is via the mirror-image space to the left. These two wedge spaces, each swooping down in a convex

arc from a height of 25 metres (82 feet), give a monumental urban feel to the building, a more elegant version of those brutal concrete interstices that are found in elevated highways, multi-storey car parks and industrial buildings all over the world. The copper-clad façade features 1.8-metre (5.9-foot) -diameter circular windows, accentuating the ship-like appearance of the structure and adding a further decorative element to the copper cladding, which has been pre-oxidized in three shades of green. The reception and bar are located on the ground floor, where an entire wall of transparent glass encourages dialogue between the lobby and the street. Above, the hotel atrium is capped by a glass-bottomed swimming pool around which the roof provides guests with an impressive observation/sun deck with views towards São Paulo's skyline.

The interior treatment necessarily responds to the innovative architectural lines of the building. There was some initial tension between Ohtake and Siaulys' choice for interior designer, João Armentano. However, Armentano, a fashionable Brazilian designer for trendy advertising agencies and of lifestyle homes for the rich and famous, proved a good choice. In any case, some of the lateral rooms could hardly avoid Ohtake's pervasive influence since their internal space is conditioned by the external arc, in some cases causing curved floors to rise up seamlessly into walls. Guest room bathrooms feature a vertically sliding divider so that guests can soak in the bathtub with a full view of the bedroom and television if they choose.

In general, with their predominance of natural materials, whites and earth tones, Armentano's interiors seem more restrained in tenor than Ohtake's architectural dramatics and there is no real dichotomy of approach. However, Hotel Unique still looks like a citadel from the outside, betraying little of what goes on within. If it is a success as the grand architectural statement Ohtake wanted, as a working hotel it is perhaps a little too ready to live up to its name. The Unique is one of a kind not just because of its visually arresting geometry but also because architects rarely, if ever, risk so challenging a hotel design except for purely polemical purposes.

ABOVE

The external lines of the hotel impose themselves on the interiors of some of the lower guest rooms – in this case, a floor segues into a wall.

LEFT

Is it a giant fruit segment? Is it a huge ink blotter? Is it a ship? Is it an ark? No, it's a hotel.

The curvilinear motif of the building is continued in the reception lounge.

LEFT
The roof deck, with its glass-bottomed pool, affords panoramic views of the São Paulo skyline.

FAR LEFT
The entrance to the hotel is through gargantuan carbon fibre doors, which give visitors early warning that Ohtake's radical exterior treatment will be followed through inside the hotel.

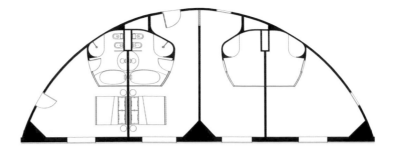

LEFT AND BELOW
The defining semi-circular profile of Hotel Unique can be seen here, repeated in the plan of some of some of its internal spaces.

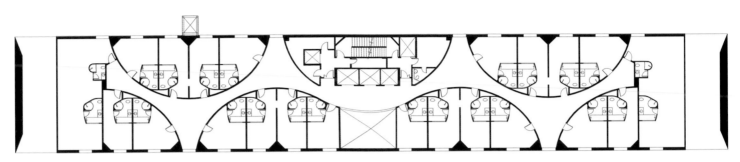

LEFT
An internal corridor defined by a series of offset, opposed curved walls.

RIGHT
A semicircular room, complete with an organic seat, for relaxing in.

Parkhotel

Hall, Austria 2003

Architects: Henke und Schreieck Architekten

One of the most unusual solutions to the problem of adapting an old hotel to modern usage is to be found in Henke und Schreieck's Parkhotel in the town of Hall, Tyrol. The original Park Hotel was designed in 1931 by Alois Johann Welzenbacher, an architect and town planner of some note and a pioneer of the Modern Movement in his native Austria. Lois Welzenbacher, as he was known, designed several private houses in the 1930s that, in their flowing curvilinear lines, revealed an indebtedness to Le Corbusier in particular and The Bauhaus in general. However, Welzenbacher's work was not always well received in his native Austria and The Park, his spa hotel set in the picturesque Alpine context of the Tyrol, was certainly not in tune with the often clichéd architecture of the region. As a result, the building's original form was criticised and greatly disfigured over the years; its cantilevered balconies, which originally gave the building a dynamic rising spiral movement, were removed and a roof pergola and *brise soleil* were also demolished. The hotel was almost pulled down on more than one occasion and various draconian structural alterations resulted in a failing edifice, no longer suitably equipped with services and not even big enough to serve as a hotel let alone as a conference centre.

Times change, however, and in 2000 three architects – Inge Andritz, Feria Gharakhanzadeh and Bruno Sandbichler – intervened to save The Park Hotel, one of Welzenbacher's last surviving buildings. They managed to galvanize local interest and a restoration competition was set up in 2001. This proved to be a confusing and ultimately indecisive exercise that resulted in the client preferring the runners-up, Henke und Schreieck's, entry over the winners, Gerold Wiederin and Andrea Konzett. The problem the architects had to solve was made even more complex by the incomplete nature of the site: the original hotel had been conceived as part of an ensemble of buildings of which one, a spa clinic, never had its intended complementary structure built at all.

Henke und Schreieck's solution was to restore the original hotel to its former glory, removing additions and replacing demolished features. Among other things they reconstructed an internal staircase and restored signature design elements such as a window in the former restaurant that can be lowered into a parapet. The guest room layout was reconfigured to match contemporary requirements but essentially the original hotel was allowed to rediscover itself in spirit, if not in every detail. Significantly, the architects then created a brand new hotel alongside the old one. The two hotel buildings, along with the spa clinic, are connected at ground level by a new building that contains the kitchen, a restaurant, a lobby and seminar rooms. At a stroke, the threat of over-adaptation was removed from Welzenbacher's building, the intentions of the original site plan were partially restored with the link building and a new, complementary hotel was created.

This new hotel building - Parkhotel - is an inverted cone, surrounded by glazing and horizontal hoops that are made of specially constructed segmental panels of powder-coated aluminium and that cast shadows on its dark-tinted glass façade. If Welzenbacher's rectilinear building invited residents to step out onto balconies and gradually descend into the bracing Tyrolean landscape, Henke und Schreieck's hotel offers panoramic views of that landscape and also of the original hotel that has now been restored. This novel solution is reminiscent of the story of the Frenchman who so loathed the newly built Eiffel Tower that he ate lunch at its restaurant every day, this being the only location in Paris from which the offending tower was not visible. At Hall, however, opposite forces are at work. Distance lends enchantment and Welzenbacher's once derided building is no longer simply a facility for viewing the natural scenery: it has itself become an honorary part of the view, something worth looking at in its own right.

LEFT

The modern and the traditional working in harmony – now linked with a new low-rise connecting building, the two contrasting structures illustrate a novel approach to modernization.

ABOVE
The two Parkhotel buildings, old and new, are connected
at ground level by a new building that contains the lobby,
seminar rooms, a kitchen and this restaurant.

NEXT PAGE
A new entrance for Parkhotel is situated in the low-rise
connecting building that seeks to complete the original
plan for the site.

RIGHT
The original pergola and *brise soleil*, long since demolished, were recreated on the rooftop of the old hotel building.

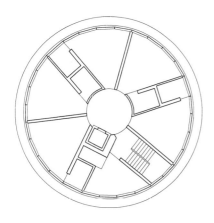

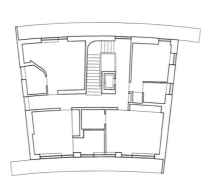

LEFT
Plans showing the shape and layout of both the new and old buildings.

ABOVE
Henke und Schreieck's restoration of the original hotel involved removing several infelicitous additions and replacing some demolished original features like this internal staircase.

ES Hotel

Rome, Italy 2003

Interior Architectss: King Roselli Architetti

Esquilino is a district of Rome for which the usual euphemism is 'colourful'. Now on its way back up from being run down, Esquilino is the focus of civic renovation and a local redevelopment scheme has been much helped by the arrival of the ES Hotel (ES being a local abbreviation for Esquilino). The district is situated in the middle of historical Rome, which soon revealed itself to be even more historical than previously thought as initial excavations revealed ancient city remains just 12 inches (30 centimetres) beneath the surface. Consequently, redevelopment plans were modified and the city council's original requirement to combine the hotel with extensive underground car parking for the area was shelved. In King Roselli's revised proposal the hotel was raised from the ground in order to allow continuing access to the historical site on one side and access to the public areas of the hotel on the other.

Out of this muddled structural beginning emerged a new hotel for owners the Roscioli family who had stipulated that they wanted a hotel 'to satisfy conscious and unconscious desires'. As a brief, this has the appeal of being entirely meaningless and so King Roselli were able to get on with the task of creating a minimalist refuge of luxury and style by means of a restrained palette of colours but with many dazzling visual effects, achieved through lighting and unexpected surfaces. Not that this achievement is necessarily well-flagged from the outside, since the external aspect of the building seems not to have been of the architects' choosing. Indeed, it owes more to the solid scale and style of the railway station that lies to its north than to the otherwise predominantly 19th century vernacular style of Esquilino. A battery of local regulations and other bureaucratic limitations inhibited the external look of the building, but once inside the architects were much freer to begin playing with shapes, spaces and finishes and they certainly made the most of the opportunity.

The reception desks in the foyer exist as effulgent organic shapes – like pulsating anemones, say the architects, although radioactive doughnuts also come to mind. The services and technological equipment that serve the conference hall are hidden inside artificial clouds; on the top level the floor peels away upwards to form service counters, while storage areas in the restaurant walls also pull away into flexible partitions.

Guest rooms are a mixture of types but all are variations on a theme. This theme places the emphasis

on the sensory effects created by the objects in the rooms, rejecting the notion of a hotel room being a home-from-home environment in favour of the unexpected. Different games are played in each type of room as space limitations have encouraged the removal of the usual barrier between bedroom and bathroom. Most usually the bathtub is enclosed in a translucent glass box that also acts as ambient room illumination. However, in more extreme cases the bath or shower is mounted on a 'raft' that is shared by a cupboard and the bed.

In what may be seen as a rather witty valedictory jab at the unavoidable multi-storey car park look of the exterior, the architects have also installed a coloured light under each window. At night, at least, the façade takes on the appearance of a luminous, multicoloured chessboard, an after-dark indicator of the dazzling effects to be found within.

ABOVE
The reception desks in the foyer are presented as glowing organic shapes – like pulsating anemones, according to the architects.

LEFT
Twin facilities in a guest room dedicated to the owners' seductively vague proposition of creating 'a hotel to satisfy conscious and unconscious desires'.

RIGHT
In some guest rooms the bathtub is enclosed in a translucent glass box that also acts as ambient room illumination.

Hotel Habita

Mexico City, Mexico 2003

Architects: Taller de Enrique Norton Arquitectos SC (TEN Arquitectos)

If the majority of new hotels are renovations or adaptations rather than new buildings, then TEN Arquitectos have blurred the distinction nicely at Hotel Habita in Mexico City. As is so often the case, demolition of an old building followed by construction of a new one attracts a wealth of planning and zoning restrictions that simply do not apply to renovations. Such restrictions are usually based on the assumption that a renovation merely tweaks what is already there. In this case, however, TEN Arquitectos have subverted the rule book and comprehensively recast an undistinguished five-storey apartment building, making its concrete-reinforced brick exterior now totally invisible behind a luminous blue-green carapace of sand-blasted glass attached with stainless steel fittings.

This is the high-profile aspect of the renovation, making a dilapidated building beautiful and insulating the new hotel visually, acoustically and also atmospherically from undesirable views, traffic noise and the city's notorious air pollution. Inside, the challenge was equally demanding since 15 apartments had to be transformed into 36 rooms and suites and a whole array of new services inserted, including light wells, elevator shafts and an air-conditioning plant. However, it is the hotel's new skin that sets the agenda for the visual treatment throughout. In an example of genuinely creative design thinking, the architect left precisely calculated clear horizontal strips in the sand-blasted glass panels of the building's new skin. These selected viewing strips had the effect of 'editing out' the least appealing parts of the view for the guests inside, while permitting only teasing glimpses into the building from outside. This strategically ambiguous use of glass as both screen and window reappears inside. A translucent, backlit check-in desk looks like an elegant vertical light box – a playful use of a material normally associated with transparency to form a screen. Behind the desk, circular stainless steel pigeon-holes form a complementary backdrop, echoing the component materials of the new façade.

The guest rooms are, necessarily, individually configured due to the rigid constraints of the internal conversion. TEN Arquitectos fine-tuned the design details in every case, customizing the built-in furniture and continuing the theme of translucent glass and stainless steel in the treatment of the bathrooms. When it comes to the balconies, the external and the internal meet as the building's new glass skin places each balcony in a transitional zone, out of the room and yet still inside the building but with the mediated views outside through the transparent slots.

Private guest facilities include an exercise room with sauna and Jacuzzi and, adjacent, the rooftop pool deck where views are once again carefully mediated by barriers and translucent glazed screens. At one end of the pool, blocking out a mundane view, is Jan Hendrix's large white-on-black ceramic mural, another attention-grabbing screening device. The roof area has two levels connected by a spiral staircase. On the upper terrace, TEN Arquitectos have again made a virtue out of a necessity by creating an open-air lounge that is protected by a lightweight tensile canopy that gets around the planning laws forbidding the building of an additional storey. This rooftop lounge, a magnet for trendy social gatherings, is equipped with a 3.5-metre (11.5-foot) -long open-air fireplace and is minimally appointed with white tile, railings of translucent glass 'planks' and a redwood floor.

Hotel Habita's design stance is unashamedly insular. It shields and protects its guests in an elegantly appointed minimalist cocoon, realised with quite exceptional taste. Next door stands a ghost of itself, a twin building that will, in time, probably be incorporated into the hotel. It acts as a reminder of the kind of shabby architecture that still exists in and to some extent defines the locale from which Hotel Habita has chosen to stand aloof. Hotel Habita is, in its own way, a gated community but one executed with such ingenuity and style that the hope must be that others will follow its lead, not resent its example.

RIGHT
On the rooftop pool deck, views are carefully mediated by translucent glazed screens and, at one end, by this large white-on-black ceramic mural by Jan Hendrix.

BELOW
An extraordinary transformation: Hotel Habita acquires a luminous blue-green carapace of sand-blasted glass panels to hide its industrial exterior and shelter its balconies.

LEFT
A bid to let some of Hotel Habita's architectural elegance spill over into the street in a district of Mexico City that has yet to become fully gentrified.

BELOW LEFT
Hotel Habita's lobby bar.

LEFT

Glass predominates in Hotel Habita. Here a translucent, backlit check-in desk looks like a vertical light box: a playful use of a transparent material to create a screen. Behind, circular stainless steel pigeon-holes echo another of the component materials of the hotel's façade.

The rooftop pool at night, with its screened guardrail neatly editing the visible cityscape.

Hotel Habita's rooftop lounge with its 3.5 metre (11.5 foot) -long fireplace, a feature designed to take the chill off a covered but otherwise open-air lounge.

Mii amo

Sedona, USA 2001

Architects: Gluckman Mayner Architects

The metaphysical recreation complex that is the Mii amo Spa contains a number of surprises. Firstly, its architects, Gluckman Mayner Architects, who are best known for their tight minimalist urban buildings, in particular their museums such as the Andy Warhol Museum in Pittsburgh and New York's Paula Cooper Gallery. Mii amo, in contrast, is a 3,159 square metre (34,000 square foot) element of the Enchantment Resort (proprietors: Sedona Managment) in Arizona's Boynton Canyon. Secondly, hotel is merely an element of the whole Mii amo experience – nobody could claim to be going to Mii amo for just a good night's sleep before driving on to Phoenix or the Grand Canyon. The accommodation is only part of a minimum three-day package (Mii amo means journey or passage in the Native American Yuma dialect) of which the main focus is a parcel of New Age healing, underpinned by the belief of generations of Apache that there is something mystical in the surrounding scenery. Thirdly, while every other hotel in the world now boasts an attached spa, the Mii amo is a spa in the middle of parched Arizona that boasts attached guest rooms.

The spa building itself is arranged along a 52-metre (171-foot) -long circulation spine – a grand hallway defined by a timber-framed roof and a terrazzo-ground concrete floor. On one side, a continuous skylight runs along its entire length; on the other are five adobe brick towers, which rise up out of the spine. The towers reference the masonry structures of Chaco Canyon and other ancient South-West American architectural sites and house what is termed 'the heart of the Mii amo experience': private rooms for massage, health treatments and relaxation.

Accommodation is in six *casitas*, block structures located within a system of interlocking courtyards, which have been integrated into an existing cottonwood tree grove. The entrances to the guest *casitas* offer a rather elegant take on traditional South-Western building vernacular with their wood trellises and synthetic stucco wall finishes. Inside, however, the guest rooms owe more to Gluckman Mayner Architects' familiar minimalist style. The firm's project architect, Dana Tang, notes that the simple objective of the guest room interiors was 'to make people comfortable and feel at home' – perhaps a sensible decision given that most other experiences at Mii amo are less likely to do so, involving as they do such things as a Crystal Grotto with a petrified tree stump fountain, Hoops & Balls classes and a yoga lawn.

The guest room interiors make generous use of wood with alder-framed platform beds and built-in night stands and closets made of the same material. In their own way the rooms are also a kind of refuge, like so many of the complex's other spaces. Lobby, library, retail area, gym, locker rooms and juice bar are all places that are dedicated to the idea of quiet relaxation. All through the complex, the architects have provided calculated glimpses and framed tableaux of Boynton Canyon's dramatic red rock landscape of bluffs and mesas. In a sense it is these surroundings that provide Mii amo's *raison d'être* and afforded Gluckman Mayner Architects the opportunity to create a sophisticated hospitality stage set for a resort that claims to provide a starting point for a journey to 'set free one's special gifts'.

The proposition is as bogus as the snake oil peddled by the salesmen who used to ply this territory a century ago, and yet Mii amo is no more than an expression of what more and more 21st century hotels seek to offer: wish-fulfilment. Here, the hotel is only a part of the package, but the exercise illustrates an increased blurring of the line between traditional bed-and-board and unashamed fantasy camp. In this instance, it is supported by superior design from a firm whose principal, Richard Gluckman, had the grace to admit at the outset that his preconception of a spa was 'an old building with hot baths and older people trying to lose weight'.

From this modest starting point the firm did in fact succeed in squaring an unlikely architectural circle: bringing their urban sensibility for galleries and installations to the great outdoors and somehow making it work in the giant landscape of the American West. As a result, Mii amo's real achievement is to have acquired an imaginative, contextual architecture to realize its fashionable, marketing-led idea.

RIGHT

The pride of Arizona's Boynton Canyon, this spectacular location was the setting for a spa complex improbably designed by Gluckman Mayner Architects, a firm best known for its minimalist urban buildings and museums.

LEFT

The entrance to the Crystal Grotto, which may sound like a Disneyland ride but does in fact manage to incorporate the distinguished touch of Gluckman Mayner in its alder wood portal.

ABOVE
A communal dining table
by Royal Custom and three
solid wood sculptures
by Tucker Robbins adorn the
complex's 52.4 metre
(172 foot) circulation spine.

LEFT
A dinette in one of
Mii amo's bamboo-floored
casitas where strong
sunlight is diffused as
it enters from above
the courtyard's high walls.

The shower area with its alder wood shelving and individual cubicles, each furnished with a slatted teak platform.

Project Credits

25hours Hotel, Hamburg, Germany
Interior Architecture and Design: 3Meta Maerklstetter + Fischer; Armin Fischer (design), Evi Maerklstetter (architect)
Project Team: Evi Märklstetter
Local Architects: Thomas Lau; Mark Hendrik Bliefferts HPV
Client: Gastwerk Hotel Hamburg GmbH
Bedroom Furniture, Flexible Bar, Wood Construction in Fire Place: Stonner GmbH
Furniture Supplier: Freiraum
Chairs in Bar and Reception: Zanotta
Sofas in Reception: Living Divani
Lighting Design: Michael Schmidt – Lichtplaner

Alila Jakarta, Jakarta, Indonesia
Architects: Denton Corker Marshall, Jakarta
Collaborator: PT Duta Cermat Mandiri
Project Team: Budiman Hendropurnomo (design principal)
Client: PT Sumbermitra Wisatagraha
Hotel Operator: Alila Hotels
General Contractor: Dimensi
Structural Engineer: PT Wiratman and Associates
Mechanical and Electrical Engineer: PT Makesthi Enggal Engineering
Art work (Lobby): Pieter Dietmar
Furniture (Lobby): DCM; Talenta
Custom Furniture (Guest Rooms): Mitra Luhur Dinamika Lestari
Lighting (Public Spaces): Gema Karya Abadi
Lighting (Guest Rooms): Maestro Lamp

Andel's Hotel, Prague, Czech Republic
Interior Design: Jestico + Whiles
Project Team: John Whiles, James Dilley, Michelle Le Masurier, François Bertrand, Johanna Stockhammer, Toby Ware, Sniez Torbarina
Client: UBM Realitätenentwicklung and WARIMPEX

Operator: Vienna International
Contractor: PORR Project

Apex City Hotel, Edinburgh, Scotland, UK
Architects and Interior Design: Ian Springford Architects
Client: Apex Hotels Ltd
Main Contractor: John Mowlem & Co. Plc
Structural Engineer: Sinclair Knight Merz
Services Engineer: RSP Consulting Ltd
Lighting Consultant: Foto-Ma Lighting Architects and Designers
Quantity Surveyor: Corderoy
Planning Supervisor: Corderoy Project Services

Clift Hotel, San Francisco, USA
Overall Design: Philippe Starck
Starck Design Studio: Brono Borrione
Client: Ian Schrager Hotels, LLC
President of Development: Michael Overington
President of Design: Anda Andrei
I.S.H. Design Studio Project Team: Kirstin Bailey, Masako Fukuoka, Dan Stewart, Melissa Sison, Lara McKenna, Kelly Behun
I.S.H. Project Coordinator: Cono DiZeo
I.S.H. Design Manager: Larry Traxler
I.S.H. Director of Graphics: Kim Walker
Project Management: Watershed Partners; Gary Klein, Bill Oster
Construction Manager: Plant Construction
Production Architects: Freebairn-Smith & Crane; Janet Crane, Javier Medina, Ian Bevilacqua
Art Installations: Gerard Garouste
Graphic Design: Baron & Baron; Fabien Baron, Lisa Atkin
Lighting Design: Johnson Schwinghammner; Clark Johnson
Landscape Design: Madison Cox

Continentale, Florence, Italy
Interior Design: Arch. Michele Bönan
Project Team: Arch. Giovanni Lombardi, Arch. Filippo Cei, Luigi Franco, Anna Maria Blower, Fiorella Gargani, Christine Hutter
Client: Lungarno Hotels
Work Direction: Arch. Nino Solazzi – Vivaengeneering srl
Construction Management: Cpf SpA
Danish Furniture: MC Selvini
Armchairs: Pierantonio Bonacina snc
Doors and Windows: Badii e Cappelletti
Whitewashing: Pennellotto Restauri srl
Lighting: Estro Illuminazione
Textiles: Blue Home SpA
Stools: Chelini SpA
Furnishings: Tappezzeria Cipriani
Bathroom Accessories: Disenia SpA
Sofas and Stools: Verzelloni
Table Lamps: Dessie'srl
Carpentry and Woodwork: Cmm
Wooden Sunblinds: Sunwood

ES Hotel, Rome Italy
Interior Architect: King Roselli Architetti
Project Team: Jeremy King, Riccardo Roselli (Project Directors); Andrea Ricci, Claudia Dattilo (Project Architects); Marina Kavalirek, Riccardo Crespi, Annalisa Bellettati
Client: C.R. INVEST srl
Design Coordinator: Marzia Midulla Roscioli
Site Supervision: Ing. Nino Bazzi
Contractors: ORION scarl; DICOS SpA
Structural Engineer: Ing. Dario D'innocenzo
AC Plumbing Electrical AC Design: SVA srl Giuseppe Vergantini
Acoustics Consultant: Biobyte srl
Furniture and Fitting Contractor: Devoto arredamenti srl; Storie srl
Lighting Equipment Supply: Baldieri srl
Curtain Walling: Edilfai
Glass Parapets in Lobby: Vetraria Federci
Furniture and Fittings: King Roselli

Additional Furniture supplied by: Cappellini, Vitra, Unifor, Sawaya and Moroni
Marble Venetian Flooring: designed by King Roselli and supplied by Marmi Menini
Reception Desk: King Roselli
Technological Clouds in the Auditorium: King Roselli
Bar: King Roselli
Curtains and Blinds: Louverdrape
Rugs: Kasthall
Audi and Video Suppliers: Sedico 84
Sanitary Ware: Giulio Cappellini and Ludovica e Roberto Palomba for Ceramica Flaminia
Sink: Montecatini 1933 designed by Gio Ponti and supplied by Rapsel
Jacuzzi Bathtubs: supplied by Albatros e Duravit
Taps: Vola by Arne Jacobsen supplied by Rapsel

ESO Hotel, Cerro Paranal, Chile
Architects: Auer + Weber + Architekten
Project Team: Philipp Auer (project architect); Dominik Schenkirz, Robert Giessl, Michael Krüger, Charles Martin
Client: ESO European Southern Observatory
Outdoor Facilities: Gesswein, Henkel + Partner
Engineering: Mayr + Ludescher (structural); HL-Technik AG (mechanical); HL-Technik (electrical); Schneidewendt (kitchen)
Lighting Design: Werner Lampl, Diessen

Four Seasons Hotel, Tokyo, Japan
Interior Design: Yabu Pushelberg
Project Team: Glenn Pushelberg, George Yabu, Christopher Koroknay, Lizette Viloria, Kelly Buffy, Ayako Sugino, Anthony Tey, Paul Pudjo, Minh Duong, Polly Chan, Sunny Leung, James Robertson, Christina Gustavs
Project Architects: Nikken Sekkei; George

Kuromado (project head); Tetsuji Yuki (project architect)
Architect of Record: Nikken Sekki, Takanaka = PCP Design Team
Client: Pacific Century Cyber Works
General Contractor: PCP Group Lighting; Cooley Monato
Engineers: PCP Group
Interior Finishes: PCP Group (acoustical ceilings and suspension grid)
Cabinetwork and Custom Woodwork: Yabu Pushelberg, Decca, Erik Cabinets
Wallcoverings, Panelling, Special Surfacing, Floor and Wall Tiles: PCP Group
Carpet: Tai Ping
Raised Flooring: PCP Group
Reception Furniture: YP; PCP
Fixed Seating: Decca
Chairs: Knoll, Palumbo, Pucci, Louis Interiors; B&B Italia; Void; Hickory
Tables: Decca, Minotti
Upholstery: McGuire, Ralph Lauren, Home, John Saladino
Downlights: Eurolight
Task Lighting: Tango
Plumbing: Dornbracht

The Gran Hotel Domine Bilbao, Bilbao, Spain
Design Concept: Javier Mariscal; Fernando Salas
Architect: Iñaki Aurrekoetxea
Client: Silken Hotels
Project Management: Vizcaína de Edificaciones SA
Graphic Design: Estudio Mariscal
Acoustics: Higini Arau
Fossil Cyprus Tree: Taller Pere Casanovas
Carpentry: Jaume Carré Sánchez
Metal Work: Talleres Colmenero
Sign Posting: Roura Cevasa
Ceramics: Jorge Fernández

The Grove, Hertfordshire, England, UK
Interior Design: Fox Linton Associates; Martin Hulbert (hotel interior); Collett Zarzycki (The Stables, Sequoia, the spa and fitness studios)
Architects: Fitzroy Robinson
Extension Architects: Scott Brownrigg Taylor
Client: Ralph Trustees Ltd
Extension Construction: Galliford Try Construction
Spa and Stable Construction: Kier Southern
Project Management: MACE; John Betty
Planning Supervisors: Faber Maunsell
Mechanical and Electrical Contractors: TBA (Troop Bywater & Anders)
Lighting: Equation
Landscapers: M.J. Abbotts
Soft Landscaping: Willoughby
Ironmongery: First Choice

Harts Hotel, Nottingham, England, UK
Architects: Marsh:Grochowski
Project Team: Mike Askey, Dan Greenway, Anke Lawrence, Julian Marsh, Mike Reade
Interior Design: Hambleton Decorating Ltd; Stefa Hart
Client: Hart Hambleton PLC; Tim Hart
Main Contractor: Marriott Construction
Services Contractor: F. G. Skerritt Ltd
Structural Engineer: Price Myers; Steve Wickman, Dan Wright
Services Engineers: D.H. Squire; Tony Harris
Quantity Surveyor: W.T. Partnership; Stuart Bates, Peter Willows
Landscape Design: Neil Hewetson
Catering Design: Gratham Winch
Planning Supervisor: Marsh Grochowski; Mike Askey
Aluminium Windows: Bonam and Berry
Steelwork: Cavill Fabrications
PC Concrete: Bison
Joinery: Winston Joinery
Furniture: Pierre Frey
Signage: Merrill Brown

Flooring: Treamar
Painting and Decoration: DKN Decorating
Glazing: Solarglas
Suppliers: Allgoods (ironmongery); 'O'
   Windows (windows and doors); Domus
   Tiles (tiling); Simas Luna, Villeroy and Boch,
   Olympus, Kaldewei (sanitary ware);
   Gaskells Broadloom (carpet); Concept Tiling
   (stone flooring); Atkinson and Kirby
   (timber flooring); Dernleys (blinds);
   Artemide, Marlin, Thorn, Crescent (lighting)

HausRheinsberg Hotel am See, Rheinsberg, Germany

Interior Design: Mahmoudieh Design
Project Team: Yasmine Mahmoudieh,
   Albino Cipriani, Ingeborg Blank and
   Heidemarie Schütz
Architects: Dr. Pawlik + Partner Gbr
Project Team: Herr Mews, Frau Bayat,
   Herr Lemmel
Client: Furst Donnersmarck; Guidotto Dr
   Graf Henckel Furst von Donnersmarck;
   Herr Schmidt (project leader)
Consultants: RWM Hotel Consult;
   Gastronomie Planung + Innovation GmbH;
   Buro Geralt GmbH; Furst Donnersmarck

HI Hotel, Nice, France

Concept: Matali Crasset with Philippe
   Chapelet, Patrick Elouardghi
Interior Design, Decoration and Graphic Art:
   Matali Crasset with the assistance of
   Christophe Thelisson, Oscar Diaz &
   Francis Fichot
Executive Architect: Frédéric Ducic
Client: HI Hotel; Joerg Boehler
General Contractor: Philippe Chapelet,
   Patrick Elouarghi, HCF sarl
Concrete Construction: Jean-Marc Lasry,
   Lasry & Moro Engineers
Bathroom Facilities and Fittings:
   Agape, Aquamass

Glass: Miroiterie Nicoise, Glasstini
Dinner Service: Manufacture de Monaco
Furniture: Modular
Furniture/Woodwork: Demichelis, Atelier
   de la Reinière, Atelier Virginie Ecorce
Lighting Consultant: Jacques Bobroff
Metalwork: L'Univers de l'Aluminium
Leatherwork/Carpets/Tapestry:
   Domeau & Pérès
Resins: Sept Résines, Mediterra Design
Sound: SES Giraudon
Hardener: Benoît B

Hotel Claska, Tokyo, Japan

Architects: Intentionallies (guest rooms);
   Urban Design Systems Co. Ltd
   (customized guest rooms, gallery, office,
   business centre)
Client: Urban Design Systems Inc
Contractors: Opus Design Studio Inc;
   Cosmos More Co. Ltd
Graphic Collaboration: Tycoon Graphics
Art Installation: Tomato
Furniture Direction: T.C.K.W. Co. Ltd

Hotel Habita, Mexico City, Mexico

Architects: Taller de Enrique Norton
   Arquitectos SC (TEN Arquitectos)
Project Team: Enrique Norten, Bernardo
   Gómez-Pimienta Aarón Hernández, Sergio
   Nuñez, Francisco Pardo, Julio Amezcua,
   Hugo Sánchez, Claudia Marquina, Carlos
   López, Martine Paquin, Adriana Díaz,
   Rubén Garnica, Miguel Ríos
Client: Hotel Habita SA de CV; Carlos
   Couturier, Moises Micha, Jaime Micha,
   Rafael Micha
General Contractor: Construcciones
   Gavaldón
Engineer: Colinas de Buen
Window Consultant: Val & Val
Graphic Design: Ricardo Salas
Art: Jan Hendrix

Model: Miguel Ríos
Computer Model: Jean Michel Colonnier

Hotel Josef, Prague, Czech Republic

Architects and Interior Design: Eva Jiricna
   Architects Ltd
Project Team: Eva Jiricna, Duncan Webster,
   Gabriel Alexander, Christine Humphreys
Collaborator: site administration, s.r.o.;
   Petr Vagner
Client: Hastalska, a.s.
Production, Electrical and Mechanical
   Drawings: g:projekt, s.r.o.
Project Management: GI-ckner Praha, s.r.o
General Contractor: Swietelsky
   Stavebni, s.r.o
Electrical and Mechanical Work:
   EZ Praha, a.s.
Lighting: Thorn Lighting CS, s.r.o.
Glass Bathrooms and Tables: Cekov
   umelecke zamecnictvi a pasirstvi, s.r.o.
Exterior and Interior Shading and Blinds:
   Cebing-Miller, s.r.o.
Interior Furniture: Snora spol. s.r.o.
Glass Staircase, Bar and Reception: Pavel
   Ruzicka – Artefakt
Curtains: Alena Kuchtova – Anna + A.

Hotel Unique, São Paulo, Brazil

Architect: Ruy Ohtake
Project Team: Ruy Ohtake, Alfred Talaat,
   Félix Araújo, Nancy Marques, Marcelo
   Jordão Armentano
Interior Design: João Armentano
Construction: Método
Acoustical Engineer: Acústica Engenharia;
   Johnson's Controls
Consultants: Alphametal (Eximax); Algrad
   Esquadrias e Fachadas Especiais Ltda; Avec
   Verre Design Produtos Especiais Ltda
Window Manufacturer: Santa Marina Vitrage
   Ltda; Penha Importadora e Distribuidora
   de Vidros Ltda; Pilkington

Garden: Gilberto Elkis
Lighting: Guinter Parschalk
Structure: Júlio Kassoy e Mário Franco
(concrete); Jorge Kurken Kurkdjian e Jorge
Zaven Kurkdjian (metalwork)
Foundation: Portela Alarcon
Installations and Air Conditioning: MHA

Ice Hotel Quebec-Canada, Quebec, Canada

Design: Ice Hotel Quebec-Canada Inc
Project Team: Denis Cantin (production
director); Serge Péloquin (artistic
director); Jacques Desbois (CEO)
Client: Ice Hotel Quebec-Canada Inc; CEO:
Jacques Desbois
Themed Suite: Dan Hanganu
Sculptors: Michel Lepire, Marc Lepire,
Louis Lavoie

Ku'Damm 101, Berlin, Germany

Art Direction/Overall Strategy, Design and
Concept: kessler und kessler
Interior Architects (Project Management):
Dipl.-Ing. Architekt Ascan Tesdorpf
Architects: Eyl, Weitz, Würmle & Partner
Architects – Redevelopment: Kadel-
Quick-Scheib
Client: HOTAKA GmbH & Co. KG
Hotel Operator: Bleibtreu Services GmbH
Design Room Furniture: Lemongras Design
Studio; Gruppe-RE
Design Public Areas for kessler und kessler:
Vogt + Weizenegger
Garden and Landscape Design: Lützow7

Le Meridien, Minneapolis, USA

Interior Design: Yabu Pushelberg
Project Team: George Yabu, Glenn
Pushelberg, Mary Mark, Reg Andrade,
Anson Lee, Eduardo Figueredo, Cherie
Stinson, Aldington Coombs, Mika

Nishikaze, Marc Gaudet, Alex Edward,
Kevin Storey, Christina Gustavs,
Sunny Leung
Architects: Antunovich Associates
Project Team: Yvonne Golds, Alistair McCaw,
Dan Whetstone, Julie Chambers
Client: James J. Graves, Graves Hospitality
Contractor: David Stark PCL/Plant
Purchasing Firm: Leonard Parker Company
Consultant: A/V Consultant, DMX Music
Lighting: Cooley Monato, TPL Marketing
Engineering: Harris Mechanical Hunt Electric
Stone Throughout: Coverings Etc Inc
Lighting Throughout: TPL Marrketing
Wallcovering Throughout:
Metro Wallcoverings
Leather Ottomans/Benches (Ground fFloor):
Kai-Leather Product Design
Wall Finish (Lobby Bar): Capriccio Arts
Acrylic Chairs/Cocktail Tables: Les Meubles
Saint-Damase Inc
Concrete Cocktail Tables: Atelier Vierkant
Art Work (Ground Floor): Umomo –
artist: Dennis Lin
Floor Lanterns: Abramczyk Studio
Concrete Artwork (Lobby Bar):
Piet Stockman
5th Floor Artwork: Paul Houseberg
Artwork Behind Reception Desk:
Hirotoshi Sawada

The Library Hotel, New York, USA

Architects: The Stephen B. Jacobs Group, P.C.
Project Team: Stephen B. Jacobs, FAIA
(project architect); Herbert E Weber Jr,
AIA (supervising principal); Sarit Shaanani
(architectural project manager)
Interior Design: Andi Pepper Interior Design
Project Team: Shufei Wu (project manager)
Client: H.K. Hotels; Henry Kallan
Main Contractor: Levine Builders

Malmaison, Birmingham, England, UK

Interior Design: Jestico + Whiles
Project Team: John Whiles, Sniez Torbarina,
Eoin Keating, Tony Ling, François Bertrad,
Johanna Stockhammer, David Archer,
Joanna Foster
Architects: Ferrier Crawford
Client: Malmaison Ltd
Main Contractor: HBG
Structural Engineer: Curtains Consulting
Engineers
Services Engineer: Buro Happold
Quantity Surveyor: Baker Hollingsworth
Associates Ltd

Mii amo, Sedona, USA

Architects: Gluckman Maynar Architects
Project Team: Dana Tang, Greg Yang (project
architects); Marwan Al Sayed, Mark
Fiedler, Carolyn Foug, Alex Hurst, Antonio
Palladino, Nina Seirafi, Michael Sheridan,
Julie Torres Moskovitz, Dean Young
Client: Sedona Resort Management
Contractor and Reception Desk: Linthicum
Engineers: Rudrow & Berry Inc (structural);
Clark Engineers (SW, MEP); Shephard-
Wesnitzer (civil)
Constultants: Ten Eyck Landscape Architects
(landscape); Sylvia Sepieli (spa); Water
Technology (pool)
Masonry: Mexican fired adobe brick
EIFS: Sto Corp
Venetian-style Plaster: ARD, Lime
Rasato Plaster
Elastomeric (TPO) Roofing: Carlisle
Syntec Systems
Aluminium Windows and Doors: Western
Insulated Glass; Brite-Vue
Skylights: Therm-O-Weld System;
Velux-America

Miróhotel, Bilbao, Spain
Architect: Carmen Abad
Interior Design: Antonio Miró with
    Pilar Líbano
Client: Mazzarredo 77
Project Management: Lantec Estudios
    y Proyectos

myhotel Chelsea, London, England, UK
Architects: Project Orange
Client: MyHotels: Owner –
    Andy Thrasyvoulou
Main Contractor: Cathedral Contracts
Project Management: Keytask
Quantity Surveyor: Gardiner and Theobold
Mechanical and Electrical Contractor: MCA
Casegoods: Andrew Thompson

Parkhotel, Hall, Austria
Architects: Henke und Schreieck Architekten
Project Team: Dieter Henke, Christian
    Farcher (project managers); Daniela
    Ferrigni, Ralf Rüssel, Felix Siegrist
Client: Stadtwerke Hall in Tirol GmgH
Site Management: BMO Baumanagement
    Oswald & Partner
Structural Consultant: Dipl. Ing. Manfred
    Gmeiner; Dipl. Ing. Martin Haferl
Environmental Service: DI Walter Prause
Mechanical Engineer: Tivoli Plan Planungs-
    und Baubetreuungs-GmbH
Electrical Engineer: Eidelpes
    Elektrotechnik GmbH
Façade: Starmann Metallbau GmbH
Roof: Walter Ploberger Isolierungen GmbH
Landscape Architects: Auböck & Kárász
Artwork/Light Sculpture: Hans Weigand
Signs: Mag. Ingeborg Kumpfmüller
Lighting Concept: conceptlicht GmbH
Lighting System: HALOTECH Lichtfabrik
Elevators: Otis GmbH

Pershing Hall, Paris, France
Interior Design: Andrée Putman sarl
Project Team: Andrée Putman, Elliott Barnes
    (principals); Jérome Clynckemaillie (senior
    designer); Linda Andrieux (stylist)
Architects: Richard Martinet Architecture
Client: LA Partners
Contractors for the Fit Out: Duriez
    Agencement (rooms); Pilot'ag
    Agencement (lobby/bar/restaurant)
Lighting Consultant: Geoff Wild –
    Extreme Latitudes
Landscape: Patrick Blanc – Garden Wall

Radisson SAS Hotel, Glasgow, Scotland, UK
Architects: Gordon Murray + Alan Dunlop
    Architects
Project Team: Gordon Murray, Alan Dunlop,
    Lucy Andrew, Maggie Barlow, Alison
    Gallagher, James Liebman, Andrew Miller,
    Karen Millar, Rory Olcayto, Stacey Philips
Client: MWB Argyle Street Ltd
Main Contractor: HBG Construction
Contractors: New Acoustics, Kevan Shaw
    Lighting Design
Quantity Surveyor: Thomas Adamson
Structural Engineer: Blyth and Blyth
Services Engineer: Blyth and Blyth
Copper Cladding: KME/TECU; John Fulton
Curtain Wall and Glazing: Henshaws
Slate Cladding: Stirling Stone
Planar System: Pilkingtons
Roofs: Miller Roofing; Sarnafil
Timber Cladding: Brynzeel/Multipanel
Glass Flooring: Haran Glass
Quarella Floors: CTD
Joiner: Jamieson Contracting
Mechanical Subcontractor: FES
Electrical Subcontractor: ELG
Lighting: Terkan
Bathroom Pods: RB Farquer
Fire Protection: Kenstallen
Ceilings: Soundtex
Fitting Out: Elmwood

Ritz-Carlton, Miami, USA
Architects: Nichols Brosch Sandoval
    & Associates Inc
Designers: Howard Design Group
Client: Lowenstein's Lionstone Hotels and
    Resorts; Flag Luxury Properties, LLC;
    Paul Kanavos

**The Sheraton Frankfurt Hotel,
    Frankfurt, Germany**
Interior Design: United Designers Europe Ltd
Project Team: Keith Hobbs, Limzi Coppick,
    Ed Price, Chris Johnston, Hildegard Pax
Architects: JSK International
Client: Hospitality Europe Services Ltd
Operator: Sheraton Management GmbH
Project Management: Hanscomb GmbH
Main Contractor: Lindner GmbH
Services Design: IB Paulus
Lighting Design: Into Lighting
    Designs Limited

Soho House Hotel, New York, USA
Interior Design: Studioilse
Creative Director: Ilse Crawford
Project Team: Sue Parker (Senior Designer);
    Many Lax (Project Manager)
Architects: Harman Lee Jablin
Client: Soho House New York LLC
Structural Engineer: James Ruderman
    Offices LLP

UNA Hotel, Florence, Italy
Architect: Fabio Novembre
Project team: Carlo Formisano, Lorenzo de
    Nicola, Giuseppina Flor, Ramon Karges
Client: UNA Hotels and Resorts
Main Contractor: Tino Sana srl
General Contractor: C.P.F
Electricity: Consorzio Artim
Air Conditioning: Gino Battaglini
Floorcovering (Hall): Pastellone Veneziano

by Collezioni Ricordi

Special Structures (Hall): Loop by Tino Sana covered with Opus Romano by Bisazza

Lighting (Hall): Modular, Chandelier by Nucleo

Seating (Hall): AND sofa Fabio Novembre for Cappellini

Floorcovering (Restaurant): Opus Romano by Bisazza

Wallcovering (Restaurant): MDF by Marotte

Special Structures (Restaurant): Tino Sano (tables); Zella (stained glass)

Lighting (Restaurant): iGuzzini

Furniture (Restaurant): Lensvelt

Special Structures (Conference Room): Cuved wall by Tino Sana

Lighting (Conference Room): Modular, RGB System by Zumtobel

Furniture (Conference Room): Fritz Hansen

Floorcoverings (Rooms): Tino Sana, laminate by Locatelli, Mosaic by Bisazza

Wallcoverings (Rooms): Leather by Cuoium

Lighting (Rooms): I Guzzini, Fibre Optics by Fort Fibre Ottiche

Furniture (Rooms): La Palma and Cappellini

Floorcovering (Corridors): gress by Cotto d'Este

Wallcovering (Corridors): Laminate by Locatelli

Special Structures (Corridors): MDF Shapes and Frames: Tino Sana

Lighting (Corridors): Modular; iGuzzini

Vigilius Mountain Resort, Meran, Italy

Design: Matto Thun

Collaborating Architects: Arch. Bruno Franchi, Arch. Renato Precoma, arch. Ulrich Pfannschmidt

Collaborating Interior Design: Arch. Christina Von Berg, Arch Gioia Gaio, Arch Dorothee Maier

Local Architect: Arch. Harry Husel

Client: Dr. Schär GmbH

Lighting: Arch. Simon Fumagalli

Graphic Support: Astrid Kampowsky,

Michaela Dehne, Sonia Micheli

Services Engineer: GMI with Studio Langer

Floor Covering: Berlinger Holzbau (larch); Grünig; Erwin Flesenbau

Walls Covering: Berlinger Holzbau (larch); Glas marthe (glass); Martin Rauch (raw clay); Merotto Milani

Ceiling Systems: Berlinger Holzbau

Lighting/Lighting Accessories: Berker, Flos, Zumtobel Staff

Furniture: B&B Italia, Baxter, Gufler, Gruber, Orizzonti, Maxalto, Merotto Milani, Moroso

Textiles: Caravane Paris, C&C Milano, Creation Baumann, Kinnasand, Kvadrat, Edmoni Petit, Frette, Rubelli, Soble Italia, Steiner, Tollgate

W Hotel, Mexico City, Mexico

Architects of Record: KMD – Mexico (Kaplan McLaughlin Díaz)

Project Team: Carlos Fernández del Valle, Juan Diego Pérez-Vargas; Maca Zeballos, Luis Bayuelo, Jesús Domínguez, Antonio Guzmán, Fernanda Ibarrola, Erica Krayer, Gabriela Martín del Campo, Vicente Peralta

Interior Design: Studio GAIA

Project Team: Ilan Waisbrod, Anurag Nema

Client: Starwood Hotels & Resorts

Project and Construction Management, Value Engineering: ADIPPSA S.A. de C.V.; Eng. Enrique Ross

Structural Engineer: BETT Construcciones; Eng Amadeo Betancourt

Plumbing and Mechanical Engineer: Sociedad Hidromecánica; Eng Sergio Herrera Mundo

Electrical Engineer: Electrical System, voice & data, CCTV, AMTV Arellano Ingeniería; Eng. Alfredo Arellano

HVAC Engineer: IACSA; Eng. José Luis Trillo

Interior Lighting Design: Johnson Schwinghammer; Clark Johnson

Exterior Lighting Design: Starco Mexico; Christian Pertzel

Kitchen and Food Service Consultant: DIPREC S.A. de C.V.; Eng. Eduardo Gómez Ceballos

Concrete Floors and Stones: Diseño Suco SA de CV

Macedonia Marble for Rooms: La Casa Del Cantero

Interior Glazing: Cristacurva

Wood Case and Custom Made Furniture: Grupo Hagan

W New York – Times Square, New York, USA

Interior Design: Yabu Pushelberg

Project Team: George Yabu, Glenn Pushelberg (principals); Mary Mack, Reg Andrade, Anson Lee, Marcia MacDonald, Cherie Stinson, Aldington Coombs, Alex Edward, Eduardo Figuerero, Marc Gaudet, Mike Nishikaze, Sunny Leung, Kevin Storey

Architects of Record: Brennan Beer Gorman Architects

Project Team: Mario LaGuardia, Kevin Brown

Client: Starwood Hotels & Resorts Worldwide

Lighting Designer: L'Observatoire; Hervé Descotte (principal)

Wall Covering, Wall Finishes: Metro Wallcoverings; Moss & Lam; Excelsor

Cabinetry, Millwork: Benchmark Furniture; Pancor Industries; Erik Cabinets

Paints, Stains: Sherwin Williams

Flooring: stone, Tile International; Sullivan Source

Lighting: Abramczyk Studio; Baldinger; Color Kinetics; Eurolite; Sistemalux; TPL Marketing; Unit Five Manufacturing

Furniture: Knoll; Minima; Pancor

W New York – Union Square, New York, USA

Architectural Design, Interior Design, Lighting Design, Furniture and Fixture Design: The Rockwell Group

Project Team: David Rockwell (president); Edmond Bakos (principal-in-charge), Alice Yiu (director of interiors); Paul Vega (project manager); Mike Suomi (senior designer); Nora Kanter, Cynthia Brooks, Kendra Sosothikul, Vincent Celano, Milagros de los Santos, Hilli Wuerz, Tomo Tanaka, Jennifer Fozo, Jeff Koo

Architects: Brennan Beer Gorman Architect; Brennan Beer Gorman Monk Interiors

Project Team: Henry Brennan, Julia Monk (partners in charge); James McMullan (project architect); Adam Brozost (job captain); Liza Crespo, Anthony Lamitola, Ernesto Acosta, Marlon Fernandez Melissa Chen with Jelena Djordjevic, Jorge Rojas (project interior)

Client: Barry Sternlicht, Starwood Capital Group

Owner: Related Lodging Group

Lighting Designer: Johnson Schwinghammer

PEP Engineers: Jaros Baum & Bolles Consulting Engineers

FF & E Contract Purchasing: Integrated Services Corp

Structural Engineer: Rosenwasser/Grossman, Consulting Engineers

Historic Preservation Consultant: Higgins & Quasebarth

Historic Archive Consultant: Office for Metropolitan History

Historic Offices: The City of New York

Environmental Consultant: ATC Associates Inc

Construction Management: Structuretone

Limestone Flooring, Pleated Concrete: Port Morris

Millwork: Mielach Woodwork

Custom Glass Leafed Panels of the Elevators: Janet Hanchey

Interior Landscaping: Flora Tech

Art/Framing: Darren Waterston through Museum Editions Art Advisors

Custom Furniture: Lambert

Custom Design Game Tables and Side Garden Tables: Unifactor Corporation

Concrete for Tables: Concrete Jungle

Leather for Tables: Dualoy

Custom Leather Wrapped Floor Lamps: Burning Relic

Leather for Floor Lamps: Moore & Gilkes

Custom Corset Lamp Shades: Blanche P. Field LLC

Decorative Dome Light Fixture: Alger International

Decorative Bobesche Fixtures: Alger International

Index

INDEX

Picture Credits

The publisher would like to thank the following sources for permission to use their images:

Arcaid – Inigo Bujedo Aquirre (6 top, 116–119); archipress – Luc Boegly (166–171); architekturphoto – Ralph Richter (5 top, 558–63); artur – Roland Halbe (122–127); Bruce Buck (106-109); Santa Caleca (2, 210–213); Xavier Dachez (110–115); Evon Dion (76–81); Alberto Ferrero (172–177); Luigi Filetici (214–215); Dan Forer (14–15 top, 16 top); Gavin Fraser (88–91); Luis Gordoai (7, 216–221); Courtesy of The Grove (24–29); Martine Hamilton-Knight (42–45); Ken Hayden (160–165); Koji Horiuchi (18–23); David Joseph Photography (5 bottom, 98–103); Ales Jungmann (30-35); kessler und kessler (52–57); Tim Kiusalaas (17); Nikolas Koenig (148-153); Nelson Kon (198–203); Jean-Michel Landecy (154–159); Andrew Lee (192–197); Albert Lim (138–141); Courtesy Mahmoudieh Design (128–131); Satoshi Minagawa (46–51); James Morris (92–97); Courtesy myhotel Chelsea (66–71); Jaime Naverro (72–75); Ivan Nemec (186–191); Augustin Ochsenneiter (132–137); Courtesy Ritz-Carlton (15 bottom, 16 bottom); Joserra Santamaría (144–147); Margherita Spiluttini (204–209); Edmund Sumner (36–41); Martyn Thompson (178–183); Rafael Vargas (120–121); Paul Warchol (82–87); Harry Zernike (222–227)

Author's acknowledgements:
The author would like to thank the following people for all their hard work in creating this book: Liz Faber, Jennifer Hudson, Lara Maiklem, Price Watkins and Kim Sinclair.